COLUMBIA UNIVERSITY ORIENTAL STUDIES

Vol. XVIII

The Chronicle of Ahimaaz

TRANSLATED WITH AN INTRODUCTION AND NOTES

By

MARCUS SALZMAN

Ahimaaz ben Paltiel

AMS PRESS, INC.
NEW YORK, N.Y. 10003
1966

THE CHRONICLE OF AHIMAAZ

NOTE

Among the few Hebrew documents of importance that have come down to us dealing with the history of the Jews in the Middle Ages—not counting the Genizah documents—the Chronicle of a certain Ahimaaz stands out prominently; and this for two reasons. In the first place it presents us with certain facts which otherwise would have escaped our knowledge. In the second place it contains some flights of the imagination which are interesting because of the light that they throw upon the spiritual history of the Jewish communities during those days. A re-edition of the text published by Neubauer is worth while because of the incomplete character of the one manuscript upon which it was based. A translation is necessary in order that they may make use of it who are unacquainted with the Hebrew language. Dr. Salzman has done both of these with much care and precision; and he has added the necessary notes in order to make plain that which may be obscure.

RICHARD GOTTHEIL

COLUMBIA UNIVERSITY,
October 5th, 1923.

PREFACE

It was with a deep sense of satisfaction that this study was undertaken. While the first suggestion of it was under consideration, interest in it was further stimulated by a note from the head of the Semitic Department in another university, independently naming the Chronicle of Ahimaaz as a choice subject of study. Now that these labors are brought to a close, I cannot but feel that such emphatic endorsement was well bestowed.

The attempts to obtain a copy of the MS. proved unavailing, but they were rewarded to the extent of receiving from Professor A. S. Yahuda, of Madrid, the personal assurance that the Neubauer edition of it is an accurate transcription of the orignal. This study of the Chronicle, like those that have preceded it, is based on the Neubauer text, but, in addition, considers the emendations suggested by Neubauer, Kaufmann, Bacher, Brody and others. The sources of the various suggestions are indicated in the notes by N, K, B and Br respectively. Through the courtesy of the Oxford University Press, the notes of its edition have here been incorporated as especially helpful in showing the condition of the MS.

The principal authorities consulted are named in the notes. Two of them have been of exceptional value; David Kaufmann, in his masterly analysis of the Chronicle (MGWJ, 1896), and Jules Gay, in an exhaustive account of the same two centuries that are covered by Ahimaaz' records, "L' Italie Meridionale et L'Empire Byzantin, 876-1071" (1904). To Professor Gottheil, to whom I owe the first suggestion of this study, I am deeply indebted for constant encouragement and scholarly guidance through the difficulties of the task. With gratitude I acknowledge also the cordial assistance of Professor J. T. Shotwell of Columbia University, of Professor Schmidt of Cornell University, and of Professor Lauterbach of the Hebrew Union College; and the efficient cooperation of Mr. F. C. Erb of Columbia Library, of Mr. A. M. Freidus of the Department of Jewish Literature of the New York Public Library, of Mr. A. S. Oko of the Hebrew Union College Library.

WILKES BARRÉ,
June, 1921.

CONTENTS

ix

THE CHRONICLE OF AHIMAAZ

PART I

INTRODUCTION

Of all the documents bearing upon Jewish History, made available in the closing years of the nineteenth century, none has been prized more highly than the Chronicle of Ahimaaz. The great expectations aroused among scholars when the first indications of the discovery of the manuscript in the Cathedral Library of Toledo by Adolph Neubauer were given by him in preliminary studies,[1] were fully realized when it appeared in a carefully edited text in his Collection of Mediaeval Jewish Chronicles.[2] It was at once acclaimed as a most valuable addition to the meager sources of our knowledge of a chapter of Jewish life that was all but closed to investigation. In the laborious attempts to piece together its story, the student's chief reliance had been the fragmentary data gleaned from the writings of Shabbethai Donnolo,[3] and from the inscriptions on the grave-stones of Venosa.[4] With such information, one could scarely avoid the summary, disdainful verdict of Graetz [5]—contrasting the wealth of evidence that proclaimed the culture of western European Jewry, with the dearth and insignificance of the records of Jewish life and learning in Mediaeval Italy, under Byzantine rule—that the period in question must have been a time of utter social degradation and of intellectual sterility, buried in oblivion because it had produced

---

[1] *JQR 4, 614; REJ 23, 236:* "Nous arrivons maintenant à un autre document qui nous donne des dates plus certaines sur notre Ahron."

[2] *Mediaeval Jewish Chronicles, II, 111–132.*

[3] An eminent physician and writer; a native of Oria, 913–982. Having traveled in quest of education among Greeks, Arabians, Babylonians and Indians, he wrote his chief work, Hakemani, a commentary to one of the leading mystical books of his day. Graetz, *Gesch. 5, 316;* Castelli *Il Commento di Sabbatai Donnolo sul Libro della Creazione;* Zunz *GV 375.*

[4] Ascoli, *Iscrizioni, 39;* Broydé, '*Paleography,' JE IX 476.*

[5] Below, *30.*

1

nothing that deserved to be remembered.   Against this positive and plausible judgment, protests that could, for the most part, be sustained only by ingenious surmise and assumption, availed but little. With the discovery of this family Chronicle, however, the discussion was no longer to be abandoned for want of tangible evidence. In it we had obtained a luminous, authentic, contemporary record that added substantially to our knowledge of the Jewish communities in the Byzantine Empire, from the middle of the ninth to the middle of the eleventh century.

In the first scholarly study of it, David Kaufmann[1] enthusiastically drew attention to its graphic account of thriving communal activity, to its direct help in establishing the identity of scholars and poets that had long been but vaguely defined in Jewish literature, to its wealth of linguistic, cultural and historical information. Bacher,[2] in the same vein, characterized it as not "une chronique sèche, mais un récit vivant, extrémement intéressant par une foule d'anecdotes historiques et toute sorte d'épisodes merveilleux."   In a review of the volume of Chronicles containing the text of Ahimaaz, Brody,[3] approvingly repeating Kaufmann's designation of it as the precious pearl of the entire collection, likewise regards it as of indisputable value. And Steinschneider,[4] controverting an opinion of Kaufmann's that the Jewish writers of Italy, for want of a sense of historical values, had contributed but poorly to the annals of Jewish life, and while believing that Kaufmann had been too lavish in his praise of the new chronicle, cites it as an instance of an important historical document written by an Italian Jewish chronicler.

This high estimate given by its first students has been confirmed in the ready acceptance and wide application of its information by their successors. Among the more recent authorities, Israel Abrahams,[5] dwells upon its special value as a personal and local chronicle, and acknowledges his indebtedness to it. Likewise,

---

[1] *MGWJ 40.*
[2] *REJ 32, 144.*
[3] *Z. der Hebr. Bibl. II 159.*
[4] *MGWJ 44, 239.*
[5] *Chapters on Jewish Literature, 213; The Book of Delight and Other Papers.*
127, 132, 305

Joseph Jacobs[1] in his survey of Jewish Historiography counts it among the chronicles of prime importance. Accepting the testimony of its traditions, S. Eppenstein,[2] in his revision of the fifth volume of Graetz' History, refutes the historian's contemptuous view of Byzantine Jewish life and culture. Again, in a study[3] of the Legend of the Four Captives, dissenting from the commonly accepted tradition of Ibn Daud[4] regarding them, he confidently rests his argument upon the narrative of Ahimaaz, which, in his opinion, is a chronicle that, to a very large extent, sheds new light upon the social status of the Jews in Southern Italy. Whereas in the earlier editions of his history,[5] Theodore Reinach sees in the Byzantine emperor Leo VI the most violent representative of administrative persecution in that mediaeval empire, in the fourth edition (1910), he has adopted the very opposite view, "Léon VI leur rendit la liberté du culte," manifestly influenced by the chronicle's unequivocal statement to that effect, a statement that we have not yet found so directly made in any other source. E. N. Adler[6] brings its information to bear upon a number of Geniza documents and submits it as decisive in determining the time and place of their origin and their documentary value. In the judgment of our foremost authority[7] in Byzantine Jewish studies, this family record is "die wundervolle Chronik." Finally, the eminent French scholar, Jules Gay,[8] in his masterly work on Southern Italy during the two centuries of Basilian sovereignty, recognizes it as an important aid to a knowledge of the Jewish Communities, better than that which we have of the Armenian and other settlements among the population of the Byzantine Empire, of whose life we have no such vivid record. Quoting from it at length, he accepts this "histoire d'une famille de notables juifs" as a trustworthy record. A collection of traditions, faithfully reflecting the life of a period that

[1] *Historiography, JE, VI 423.*
[2] *Gesch. 5, 332, note 1.*
[3] *MGWJ 55, 622.*
[4] Sefer haKabala (Neubauer, *MJCI, 67;* Abrahams, *J.Lit. 213*).
[5] *Histoire des Israélites, 1901, 43.*
[6] *REJ 67, 40.*
[7] Krauss, *Studien zur byzantinisch-jüdischen Geschichte (1914), 43.*
[8] *L'Italie méridionale et l'Empire Byzantin (867–1071), (1904), 591.*

was so largely a *terra incognita* of historical study, may well have been considered a particularly happy discovery, Revelling in the possession of this treasure, Kaufmann[1] truly thought of it as the large fulfillment of a wish long cherished by scholars, hoping against hope that their suspicion of vigorous life among the Jews of Byzantium would, by unquestionable testimony, grow into conviction.

The author unpretentiously named his work, "A Book of Genealogies."[2] The title gives but little indication of its exceptional worth. Even a cursory reading of it proves that it is by no means an arid chronicle of men and events such as is usually suggested by that designation. With striking literary skill, the *disjecta membra* of ancestral traditions are assembled in a vividly interesting and instructive story. No doubt, as the author says, the material had to be laboriously "gathered like stubble,"[3] but the remarkably coherent product he has made of it gives no impression of a halting and crude narrative. The invocation, and the introductory statement of his aim, with his pledge of accuracy, are the index of a mind that is wholly aware of the difficulties of its task, yet reverently confident of its ability to overcome them, for the exaltation of the departed sages, and for the edification of their descendants. And for this labor of love nothing but the most artistic setting, as it was understood in the author's day, will suffice. By the use of the rimed prose structure,[4] so highly favored at that time, he added to the difficulty of setting forth the annals of his family; imposing its artificial literary restraints and demands, it is probably responsible for an occasional inaccuracy in the details of the record.

Donnolo,[5] a century before Ahimaaz, had already made use of

---

[1] *MGWJ 40.*

[2] Below, *60.*

[3] Below, *60.*

[4] Bacher *REJ 32, 147*, observes on its literary form, "généralement écrite dans une prose rimée assez aisée et claire, et qui ne rappelle la langue de Kalir que par quelques irrégularités et quelques formations de mots très hardies." A unique form, as noted by Neubauer, "étant écrite en prose rimée est impossible à traduire en Français," (*REJ 23, 236*).

[5] Above, *1* note 3.

this distinctively Arabic form of writing, in the introduction to his "Hakemani." During this century the exotic model of the Maqamat [1] continued to grow in favor among Jewish writers, especially after new impetus had been given to the fancy for it by the popular works of the Arabian Al Hamadhani,[2] a forerunner of Hariri,[3] who, a hundred years later, developed this literary form to its highest degree of excellence. When this chronicle of Oria was written, in the middle of the eleventh century, this co-ordination of Hebrew idiom and Arabic structure had become characteristic of Byzantine Jewish literature. Arabic influences had not then shattered the power of Hebrew as a living tongue. There is no indication of indifference to it, such as impelled Alharizi [4] to rebuke his contemporaries. The prevailing contempt for the language of the Bible is vividly brought home to him, when the work of Hariri is hailed by the Jews as a unique treasure. He determines to show by his translation of Hariri's anecdotes, and by his own "Tachkemoni," the equally impressive possibilities of the Hebrew language, and to trace the ingenious parables and sublime thoughts to their source in Jewish tradition. There is, manifestly, no ground for such lamentation in Ahimaaz' day. The free use of the good cultivated in the literature of others is thought compatible, in these mediaeval Jewish communities, with intelligent adherence to the excellence of their own. In the selection of the rimed prose form, Ahimaaz was

[1] "The word maqama (lecture or séance) had long been used to describe the gatherings of the learned men and poets clustered about the Caliphs and Governors, at which they exchanged ideas on grammatical points, and vied with one another in wit and erudition." Huart, *History of Arabic Literature* (1903), *133*.

[2] This Arabian writer, surnamed the wonder of his time, flourished about the latter half of the tenth century. Through his letters in rimed prose, on literary topics, he gave new vogue to this form of writing. "To him belongs the credit of having created a new form of literature, by making a volume of short stories of the comic adventures of beggars and rogues, painted in the most brilliant colors by a learned author."—Huart, *134*.

[3] Improving upon the work of Al Hamadhani, Al-Hariri (1054–1122) produced the masterpiece in the rimed prose maqama literature, in his brilliant collection of stories (50) with their "fictitious hero, a vagabond nursed on literature, called Abu Zaid of Saruj" (Huart, *ib.*).

[4] Abrahams, *J.Lit. 131*; Karpeles, *Jewish Literature and Other Essays, 210*; Graetz, *6, 209*; De Sacy, *Journ. As.* (*1833*), *306*.

no doubt governed by something more than his individual preference. It may reasonably be supposed that there was a popular demand for it. Its use could not have been altogether arbitrary, adopted in a spirit of pedantry, to make an empty show of versatility. Some general acceptance of the chronicle must have been intended. There must have been an appreciative reading public that the author had in view. It is the public of those Byzantine Jewish communities that was distinguished for its encouragement of the sacred poetry of the Paitanim,[1] and whose intellectual capacity Ahimaaz, one of its poets, must have known. Furthermore, his work must have won the favor of its first readers; that public verdict of approval may well have stimulated the judgment of the copyist, who thought it worthy of being copied. It is a substantial, artistic product, worthy of the accomplished scholar and poet that the author was.

To the Arabic literary refinement that so largely suggested its form must be added the influence of the Greek environment that likewise aided in its construction, with its language, and its popular literary devices. The double alphabetical acrostic of the elegy that serves as a closing impassioned survey of the family record, and the more important nominal acrostic that reveals the author's name, are modeled after well-known forms of Byzantine Literature. Regardless of what may be said of the original source of the acrostic,[2] whether it was borrowed from Greek or

---

[1] The earliest liturgical poet of the synagog of whom we have knowledge is the Palestinian Jose ben Jose, of the 6th century. His most famous followers, of a century later, were Jannai, and Kalir. The latter was the first to embellish the entire liturgy with a series of hymns whose essential element was the Haggadah, and gave his name to that form of elegiac poetry, with its "profusion of rare words and obscure allusions, which was favored by the prolific Byzantine Jewish poets, and was adopted by the communities of France, England, Burgundy, Lorraine, Germany, Bohemia, Poland, Italy, Greece and Palestine. Whereas in Spain, the form more truly poetic, both in structure and in idea, developed in Castile, Andalusia and in countries where Arabic influence was strongest." Zunz, *Literaturgeschichte; 26, 28, 29;* Dukes, *Ehrensäulen und Denksteine;* Berliner, *Die Juden in Rom, II 15;* Abrahams, *J.Lit., 83ff;* Deutsch, *JE X 65.*

[2] Zunz, *GV 391, 397;* Krumbacher, *Geschichte der byzantinischen Literatur, 697;* Abrahams, *J.Lit. 83.*

from Syriac Literature, there was a conspicuous development of such poetry in Byzantium. Its frequent use among Hebrew writers seems to begin with the Geonic age; during that period it was assiduously used by the Byzantine writers, above all, the hymnologists;[1] there was a general fondness for it among the people. As a standard of acceptable writing in his day, it must have impressed Ahimaaz; in the atmosphere in which the acrostic flourished so luxuriantly, he must have found strong incentive to make use of it. We may also reasonably see in the very conception of this Hebrew chronicle the direct influence of the host of annalists, chroniclers and historians of the Byzantine world. The freedom of movement among the peoples of the empire could not have left him unaffected. He must have submitted to the influences that centered in Constantinople, then the first city of the world. That he is a keenly observant man of letters is beyond question. He must have availed himself of his opportunities to have first-hand knowledge of Byzantine life and literature. Whether, as Kaufmann[2] seems to believe, no written family records were transmitted to Ahimaaz, or, more probably, some poorly preserved documents were at his disposal, he finds the need of supplementing the fragments of tradition with copious notes.[3] In these explanatory passages there is ample evidence that he has had access to other sources of knowledge, in all probality, Byzantine sources, by means of which he has transformed the meager annals into a fluent narrative.

But the peculiar literary mould into which the chronicle has been cast is all but overlooked in the interest awakened by its substance. From the very beginning, one observes that

---

[1] Of the development of the sacred poetry of the Byzantine church, Krumbacher says, "Die eigentliche Hymnendichtung beginnt wahrscheinlich im 5. Jahrhundert. Sie blühte besonders im 6. und 7. Jahrhundert. (Die kunstvoll ausgeführten, grossartigen Gesänge eines Romanos und Sergios). Im 11. Jahrhundert ging die Blühte der Hymnendichtung zu Ende" (677). His criticism of the poets of the period of deterioration is, "Eine gemeinsame Eigenschaft dieser Dichter ist schwülstige Breite die, namentlich durch massenhafte neugebildete Beiwörter bezeichnet, häufig in leeres Wortgepränge ausartet." See also Dieterich, *Gesch. der byzantinischen und neugriechischen Literatur*" (1902), *30, 32.*

[2] *MGWJ 40, 540.*

[3] Below, *60.*

the author makes no discrimination between legend and history.
We look in vain for a selective rationalizing mind at work upon
the traditions. From the standpoint of radical historical
criticism, a document betraying such antiquated crudeness,
thereby condemns itself as worthless in the service of modern
historical study, doomed to be counted among the collections of
garrulities and stupidities[1] of the Dark Ages. But such criticism
must surely yield to the more plausible view that pleads the
author's right to be judged by the standard of his own time.
Historiography,[2] in the broader sense, recognizes no such dead
line against the writings that, in their naïveté, reflect truly the
thought and life of centuries.

The work of Ahimaaz, the child of his age, is, all in all, a
legitimate product of the mediaeval "âme neuve et naïve."[3]
He draws no sharp line of distinction between the fantastic traditions of the supernatural and the bald annals of reality. Hered-
ity and environment were at one in fostering the mentality that
found the miraculous deeds of saints and masters of secret lore
no less acceptable and credible than the more tangible achievements of statesmen and conquerors. The life of St. Nilus,
"le chef-d'oeuvre de la hagiographie calabraise,"[4] typical of the
many lives of the Saints, scarely more than a collection of stories
of sorcery, of miraculous healing, of wonders done by the saints,
is a work of biographical and historical importance. And the
writers of professedly historical records are aptly described as
"chroniqueurs byzantins toujours grands amis du merveilleux,"[5]

---

[1] Sandys, *History of Classical Scholarship I, 427*. The opinion of Ogg
(*Source-book of Mediaeval History, 934*), regarding the narrative of Ammianus,
that it is invaluable in spite of digressions and speculations on utterly foreign
topics, is quite generally applicable to the mediaeval sources.

[2] J. T. Shotwell, *History, En. Br. XIII*. Berthold Lasch, *Das Erwachen und
die Entwickelung der historischen Kritik im Mittelalter (6–12 Jahrhundert), 1887*.

[3] Jaulmes, *Essai sur le Satanisme et la Superstition au Moyen Age, 1900*.
Ellinger, *Das Verhältniss der öffentlichen Meinung zu Wahrheit und Lüge,
1884*. Gebhart, *De l'Italie mystique, 1893*.

[4] Gay, *L'It. merid. 269, 278;* Lasch *117*, "Lange Zeit herrscht den Wundern
gegenüber völlige Kritiklosigkeit, nicht blos in den Heiligen-Biographien.—
Gregor von Tours schweift fast auf jeder Seite seiner Frankengeschichte
in ausführlichen Wundererzählungen ab."

[5] Vogt, *Basile 1 et la Civilization byz. à la fin du 9. s., 26*.

as we should expect of those who studied and recorded with and for the mediaeval mind of the Empire of the East. In the prophecies, prodigies and miracles that Finlay[1] singles out for observation in the chronicles of Theophanes, and the other biographers of Leo the Isaurian, they are representative of the age. Nor is this unreserved acceptance of the supernatural confined to the masses and the writers of average learning and ability; in the ranges of exceptional intellectuality also, a Photius[2] and a Psellus[3] do not discriminate against it. Another point of close resemblance between the material in this chronicle and that of similar works of contemporary Byzantine writers, is the marked contrast between the fullness and assurance with which the legends of the marvelous are told, and the brevity and indifference that obscure the stories of fact.

Beyond these general considerations regarding the substance of this record, special interest attaches to its scope, covering almost exactly the two eventful centuries between the rise of the Macedonian dynasty[4] in the Byzantine Empire and its fall. It bears directly upon the epochal years that began with the accession of Basil, the Macedonian groom and soldier of fortune; the usurper of the tottering throne of Michael the Drunkard, to whom it was given to save the state from imminent disintegration, and to inaugurate a new day of commanding splender and power; the founder of the dynasty, under whose sovereigns the Byzantine Empire reached the height of its prosperity between the middle of the ninth and the middle of the eleventh centuries. The year in which Ahimaaz finishes his chronicle, 1054, antedates by a few years the time in which Theodora,[5] the last scion of the Basilian dynasty, comes to the throne; heir to an empire rapidly yielding to the forces of dissolution, and finally doomed when Michael VI, succeeding to

---

[1] Finlay, *History of Greece, II, 25*.

[2] Sandys, *I, 388ff*.

[3] Rambaud, *Michel Psellus, Revue historique 3, 241*. Rhodius, *Psellus*. Sandys, *I, 401*; Krumbacher, *168, 628, 721*.

[4] Finlay, *II, 228*; Vogt, *Basile 1*; Gibbon, *ch. 48*; Hartmann, *Gesch. Italiens im Mittelalter III, 1 Hälfte, 268*. Constantine Porphyrogenitus, *Vita Bas.*

[5] Finlay, *II, 447*.

power after her death, surrenders the imperial crown to Isaac Comnenus,[1] the leader of the rebellious Byzantine nobles of Asia Minor. It marks the inglorious close of a chapter of vital importance in history, that opened with a hundred years [2] of the consolidation of legislation and despotism under the first four emperors, that rapidly advanced to a culminating period of conquest and military glory (963–1025), and that hastened to its end, through a brief period of feeble administration, the conservatism and stationary prosperity under Constantine and the three consorts of the Empress Zoe, "when intelligent centralization had passed into stupid despotism," [3] (1025–1054), and prepared the way for the conquests of the Norman invader.

The chronicle, purporting to confine itself to the inner affairs of a Jewish family extending over that period, naturally drawn into the currents of the tumultuous life that surrounded it, could not well be an utterly detached document, showing no point of contact with the men and the events that shaped the history of Basilian sovereignty. The author's first complete tradition dates from the time of Basil I. The general initial statement in which he traces the remote origin of his family in Oria to the exiles of Judea whom Titus brought to Italy, seems to have been the prevailing opinion among the Byzantine Jews during the period of which he writes, as the same view regarding the first Jewish settlements is expressed in the Josippon,[4] written almost a century earlier than the work of Ahimaaz; probably it was still the commonly accepted belief in the chronicler's day. He would then be justified in attributing such a tradition to his ancestors, to add to the completeness of his story, even if he had no specific family record of it. This would seem to be substantiated

---

[1] Chalandon, *Essai sur le Règne d'Alexis 1 Comnène.* Curtis, *Roger of Sicily*. Haskins, *The Normans.* Delarc, *Les Normands en Italie.* J. B. Bury, *Roman Emperors from Basil II to Isaac Komnenos (English Historical Review, 1889).* Chalandon, *Histoire de la Domination Normande en Italie et en Sicile.*

[2] Sandys, *I 401.*

[3] R. C. Jebb, *Modern Greece, 24.*

[4] Joseph b. Gorion, commonly known as Josippon, was the author of a history of the Jews from the fall of Babylon (538 B.C.E.) to the fall of Jerusalem (70 C.E.). He was probably a native of Southern Italy, in the latter half of the tenth century. Abrahams, *J.Lit. 214; Zunz, GV 154ff, 376;* Graetz, *5, 251.*

by the fact that he has no word of private tradition regarding
the eight centuries intervening between that time of settlement
on the soil of Italy and the time of Amittai, the first of his progeni-
tors of whom he can speak with any degree of certainty, so that he
must content himself with the assumption, truly warranted, that
the years hidden in obscurity were not barren years, but richly
productive of vigorous and thriving life that made possible the
career of this distinguished figure in the ancestral line. And of
this ancestor, emerging in the middle of the ninth century, his
information restricts him to but a dim outline.

It is indeed noteworthy that any Jewish family could so clearly
have traced its pedigree through two hundred years of the
Middle Ages. Yet, when we consider that in this instance, the
starting-point is found in the reign of Basil I., we might question
whether it is by mere coincidence that the light fails the author
beyond this point. There must have been a dead-line, baffling
all penetration, fixed by the forces of disorder that were rampant
until the organizing and saving power of Basil subdued them.
For many years[1] before the establishment of the Macedonian
regime, there had been notoriously vicious adminstration and
consequent social degradation. Harassed by the Saracens from
without, distracted by anarchy within, the empire had come to
the verge of dissolution. During the more than one hundred
years between the fall of the exarchate of Ravenna and the reign
of Basil, there had been almost incessant antagonism and warfare between rival ducal interests. "Occupés à batailler,"[2] says
Gay, "les uns contre les autres, quelle resistance peuvent-ils
opposer aux Sarrasins? Les guerres privées, que deviennent
pour ces seigneurs turbulents et féroces, une habitude et un besoin,
font autant de ravages et amènent autant de ruines que les
incursions musulmanes. C'est l'anarchie féodale dans toute
son horreur." The recovery of Byzantine power and prestige,
under Leo the Isaurian[3] and his Iconoclast followers, had been
succeeded by a deterioration that was at its worst stage under the

[1] A century of tumultuous vicissitudes from the fall of the exarchate of
Ravenna to the accession of Basil (866). Finlay, *II, 43*.
[2] Gay, *69*.
[3] Finlay, *II, 13*.

impotent Michael[1] the Drunkard, the immediate predecessor of Basil. Furthermore, the province of Apulia was the specially coveted objective of the Arabian invaders; it had been the scene of fierce battles, until it fell into their hands (849–866). Under such conditions there could have been no security for any material gathered for private record; there could have been no encouragement to gather it. The populous Jewish settlements in this province lay directly in the path of the plundering hordes. Few intelligible records could have survived, even if they could have been coherently written, amid such havoc of invasion, deportation and decimation. Ahimaaz was not likely to find any family tradition of those earlier ancestors, of whom all trace was, for the time being at least, completely lost. But what was then denied to Amittai and his descendants, may through the perseverance of modern scholars be granted to us. Among the manuscripts of the Geniza in his possession, E. N. Adler[2] has found a letter that seems to lead a little further through the obscurity of that troublous period. Its reference to an Amittai b. Hodia, whom he seems correctly to identify with the patriarchal ancestor of Ahimaaz, would give us the additional knowledge of an older generation of the line of descent.

Under Basil a new day of aggressive and constructive energy begins. Royal favor bestowed upon the wisest son of Amittai, saves at least his own community at Oria, and probably, as was believed by the Jews of the Middle Ages,[3] a number of neighboring ones, from oblivion. The recollection of such an experience and of the hero to whom it was due was in little danger of being lost; and with a naturally vivid impression of the communal life in which he grew to leadership, tradition would here clearly determine for the chronicler where the actual history of the family should begin, with the material at his command. It would certainly be treasured as a thrilling topic of oral and written transmission. That the immediate family of Amittai had no knowledge of anything like it, by which an earlier branch of the family might have been remembered, must also have contributed to the de-

---

[1] Finlay, *II, 161.*
[2] Adler, *REJ 67, 40.*
[3] Graetz, *5, 245.* Bacher, *REJ 32, 144ff.* Krauss, *Studien, 44.*

termination of the beginning of the family record. The position
here taken presupposes that Ahimaaz depended largely upon written sources for his information; not so much upon formal collections of traditions, as upon brief notes of interest to the family
made from time to time by his ancestors, sages and poets, who
might be expected to give attention to some such record, or upon
their writings and those of their contemporaries that would surely
reflect the leading facts of their experience. What may at one
time have been sufficient material for a complete history of
the family, had come down to Ahimaaz as a confused mass of
fragments. He found it so incomplete that, as Kaufmann remarks, he could not, as a rule, give any chronological information
about his family.

Upon closer study the intrinsic value of the Chronicle is
more clearly seen. To begin with, the biographical notes it
contains compel attention. If it had given us nothing more
than the bare enumeration of the respective heads of the eight
generations which it sets in order, it would have done much
to clear up a number of difficulties, that have encumbered Mediaeval Jewish studies in general, and Byzantine Jewish research
in particular. At the head of the ancestral line, Amittai is all
but forgotten, not even his father's name is remembered; tradition has preserved his name and the recognition of his eminence as a master of talmudical learning and a liturgical
poet. But even this incomplete tradition serves as an indisputable corrective of the speculations about the facts of his
life. The family annals are much more circumstantial regarding
the distinguished sons of this patriarch. The eminence, especially recognized in their day, the mastery of secret lore
and its practice, is recalled at great length, but not to the exclusion of their renown as leaders of the people in school and
synagog, sages and poets, through whose quickening labors,
Oria was a center of Jewish learning. The traditional estimates
of the greatness of the three brothers are clearly indicated.
Eleazar, the youngest, who is very briefly mentioned, yet
honored for high attainments, is evidently not ranked with the
two elder brothers. The story proceeds from the less to the

more eminent, quickly disposing of Eleazar; for a while mingling
the copious traditions of Shephatiah and Hananeel; exalting
them with equal praise, but finally elevating Shephatiah above
them all. This part of the Chronicle not only added a new
name to our list of liturgical poets, but also dispelled all doubt about
the time and the country in which Shephatiah[1] and Hananeel[2]
lived, and proved that in this Shephatiah we had the original
of the heroic figure of Mediaeval Jewish legend.

The Chronicle did not rigidly confine itself to the mem-
bers of this family; mingled with this information was the
story of the far-reaching influence of Abu Aaron,[3] the Babylonian, in his travels among the communities of Southern Italy;
a story that revealed for the first time the real master who
had long been a legendary Father of Mysteries, counted among
the fantastic creations of the mystical mind. In the same
comprehensive way, considerable space is given to a tradition
about one of the leading poets of that early generation, Silanus,[4]
whereby we can replace vague theory with substantial truth as
to his place in the succession of the synagog's liturgical poets.
Again, the Chronicle's facts regarding the family's most conspicuous representative in the third generation, Amittai[5] b. Shephatiah,
remove all uncertainty as to when and where he appeared in our
literary history. As the family record unfolds we see what good
reason there is for the joy that the chronicler manifestly finds
in his labor. These descendants of the first Amittai are, with
the single exception of the unworthy Baruch, true to their high
heritage of learning and piety. They were not all poets and
teachers; some of them were famous men of affairs, called to high
adminstrative office in the state. Intense interest attaches to
the wealth of tradition setting forth the unique greatness of
Paltiel, who rises to the dignity of vizier of Al Muizz,[6] the first
Fatimite caliph of Egypt. Similar distinction is bestowed
upon the author's grandfather, Samuel, the Minister of Finance

[1] Below, *62, 81;* Zunz, *GV 376;* Graetz, *5; 245.*
[2] Below, *62, 77.*
[3] Below, *63, 76;* Neubauer, *REJ 23, 236.*
[4] Below, *68.*
[5] Below, *86.*
[6] Below, *88.*

in the principality of Capua, and upon his son, Paltiel, the author's father. In marked contrast with this eager, extended narrative devoted to a Paltiel,[1] is the brevity with which others, who must have been less renowned, are entered in the record. This was partly due, no doubt, to such discrimination shown in the material at the author's disposal, expressing the judgment of his ancestors on the more and the less eminent; the independent judgment of Ahimaaz also, may well be partly accountable for it. A compiler of literary insight and of a keen sense of proportion, he may have said even less than he could have said of a Hasadiah[2] and others who appear only in name, who seem to be hurried over so that the more illustrious career may be the more quickly reached, and that the most may be made of every incident bearing upon it. Finally, not the least important item in these biographical notes is that which gives us some actual knowledge of the author himself,[3]—born in Capua in 1017, writing his chronicle in 1054; eventually returning to the home of his ancestors, Oria. In this crowning work of his life, Ahimaaz ben Paltiel reveals himself as the elegiac poet who had long been a problem to the historian of Jewish Literature.

From this survey of the chronicle's biographical data, it is evident that the author did not content himself with a loose array of the gleanings in his possession. Pedantic compilation and transcription, rigidly confined to the source in the rough, could not have produced this work. The freedom of thought and language characteristic of a Paitan, has here been used to good purpose, so that the intention to do justice to the facts, by means of ample comments and connectives, is carried out. In some instances the supplementary information is easily distinguished. A badly shattered body of tradition could not well have preserved, in such complete form, the detailed description of Al Muizz' expedition to Egypt,[4] and that of the lavish magnificence of the caliph's palace and the incidents of

[1] Below, *88.*
[2] Below, *88.*
[3] Below, *100.*
[4] Below, *93;* Amari, *Storia dei Musulmani di Sicilia, 2, 281.* Müller, *Der Islam* (1885), *1, 618ff.*

the visit of the Byzantine envoy,[1] as anecdotes of the life of Paltiel. Similarly, the attempt at chronology at the end of the Chronicle gives the impression that there is very little in the record by which it may be accurately determined. As he was about to finish his task, the author may have felt that some such scheme of years, at least approximately accurate, filling a void in the traditions, could be developed out of what was to be inferred from them and what could be derived from other sources of information. There is in the crude annals some reliable guidance for the student of their chronology. Unmistakable historical landmarks along the line of succession, may well have seemed sufficient, in the judgment of the guardians of the record, to tell the number of their years. The time of the first generation is quite accurately determined when we read of their experiences in the reign of Basil,[2] described in terms that can apply only to the first Byzantine emperor by that name. And the succeeding generations are marked off by points of contact with the men and the events that helped make Byzantine history during the two hundred years of the record.

These family memories, then, interesting as they are to those to whom they are of immediate concern, also have distinct value for their thoughts on the general history of the world in which the men and women of this family circle moved. In them, we have for the first time contemporaneous attestation of Basil's missionary zeal against heretics in general and the Jews in particular, from a new point of view. Their intrepretation of this policy of the Emperor as one of cruel fanaticism is, of course, the very opposite of that which is common to the Byzantine chroniclers, who regarded such persecution as a wise and praiseworthy exercise of imperial power. There is but one of them, Zonaras, who denounces Basil as an "ignorant and superstitious bigot." This dissenting view, however, could scarely prevail as against that of the men who wrote under the dictation of the

---

[1] Finlay 2, 208; Weil, 2, 297; Amari, Storia, 2, 279; Gay, 158; Theophanes Contin. 60; Symeon Magister, 419; Genesios, 29; Leo Grammaticus, 452; Below, 89.

[2] Below, 69, 73.

royal biographer of Basil, his grandson Constantine Porphyrogenitus. Such exaltation, sustained by the conciliation of the
Pope, by extensive building of churches, by zeal in converting
Jews, was likely to be recorded, to the exclusion of the less flattering
testimony. It may well be, as Finlay concludes, that "though he
was a judicious and able sovereign, he has been unduly praised,
because he was one of the most orthodox emperors of Constantinople in the opinion of the Latin as well as of the Greek
church." In this connection, it should be observed that the
chronicle of Oria qualifies its bitter denunciation with a report
of the good that it knows of him. In this spirit of justice, we are
told that Basil was indeed the author and the administrator of the
monstrous edict of persecution, but he was not lost to all sense of
honor and gratitude. His pledge to the sage of Oria is scrupulously
kept, though it means a decided lapse from his highest ambition.
Lamentation over the years of his intolerance does not crowd out
the recognition of the noble act that illumines the record of
violence. With this tradition of Ahimaaz before him, Graetz[1]
could have said with greater assurance: "Basil is not to be
counted among the most depraved of Byzantine sovereigns;
he was not utterly lost to the sense of justice and clemency."

This chronicle stands alone in its reference to a daughter[2] of
Basil. Inasmuch as the leading Byzantine annalists and historians are actually official recorders, chiefly interested in affairs of
state, they would naturally confine themselves to the consideration of men and women who held some position of political,
ecclesiastical or military importance. That they make no mention of a daughter of this emperor would, therefore, not
warrant discarding the Jewish tradition as untrustworthy. The
presumption in its favor is strong; a presumption based upon the
remarkable accuracy of the chronicle in the passages that can
be controlled by the traditions of established authority. In this
respect, the entire passage of which the story of the emperor's
daughter is a part, is a typical instance. What we have learned
from the official sources regarding Basil's methods of bringing

[1] *Gesch. 5, 244.*
[2] Below, *71.*

the Jews into the church [1]—the ensnaring religious disputation, the use of suasion through the promise of freedom from indignities, and exemption from extortionate taxation, and the assurance of appointment to positions of honor, and, as a last resort, the violence of compulsory baptism,—is here told in the concrete experience of Shephatiah, the unsuspecting Jewish sage, escaping the snare of the discussion of the surpassing splendor of Saint Sophia, resisting all efforts to tempt him to abandon his faith with the allurements of lavish wealth and honors; and finally, awakened to the sinister purpose of all the attention bestowed upon him, insisting upon his dismissal, the protection granted him under the royal seal alone saves him from the violence to which the emperor is aroused. And this agreement with the accepted records of that period extends even to the name of the favorite imperial villa Bukoleon, and to the obtrusiveness of the images, which is implied in Shephatiah's insistence upon a place of seclusion, free from them. Whether these details were so fully transmitted in his family fragments, or drawn from the author's own fund of current knowledge, his presentation of them reveals an accurate recorder.

It is, however, a trial of our faith in him as he advances in the history of the Empire and differs from all other sources in what he emphatically ascribes to the successor of Basil, Leo VI.[2] Apparently yielding to a strong temptation, Ahimaaz has placed in juxtaposition, the contrasting traditions about Basil and Leo: for the moment he disarranges the story of Shephatiah, and confuses the sequence of events. As opposed to the oppression of Basil, the toleration of Leo, so gratefully remembered, may well have served to stimulate the chronciler's eagerness to turn to this bright page of the record. To his ancestors and to him, it is the outstanding fact of the reign of the second emperor of the house of Basil, this annulment of the edict of persecution. All in all, this tradition, whose terseness is but a poor measure of its unique importance, was aptly inserted where it was least likely to mar the coherence of the chronicle. In attributing

---

[1] Constantine Porphyrogenitus, *Vita Bas. XCV, 357;* Vogt, *Basile 1, 302 ff.;* Krauss, *Studien, 44;* Below, *72.*

[2] Below, *74.*

to him the restoration of their religious liberty, there is the clear
thought of his complete and individual possession of the throne.[1]
No such doubt enters here as has arisen from the conflict of
authorities on this point. However, as between those who contend
that he ruled jointly first with his elder brother, before their
father's death, and later with the younger, until the latter,
wearying of imperial responsibility, yielded all power to Leo, and
those who see no evidence of joint sovereignty, modern historians
designate the period of Bzyantine history between 886 and 912
as the reign of Leo the wise, or the Philosopher, as Ahimaaz does.
Equally explicit is the chronicle's designation, in the phrase
"his own flesh," of Leo as the son of Basil. It betrays no trace
of the suspicion, to say nothing of the actual belief, that he was
the son[2] of the murdered Michael III, the view generally held
by modern historians, accepting the testimony of the principal
Byzantine chroniclers, finding conclusive proof of its validity
in their report that Leo, immediately upon his accession, dis-
interred the body of Michael, to honor it with the royal burial
that Theodora and Basil had denied it. Ahimaaz' testimony on
such matters may fairly be judged as the opinion of those who
had scant means of going back of the realities of their time.
To them, his immediate and uncontested succession to Basil
may well have been sufficient reason for considering him a legitimate son. Likewise, to all appearances, he was sole ruler,
even though his brother may also have been emperor in name.

The fervid invocation of blessing, inspired by the memory of
Leo,[3] demands special consideration. It clashes, at every point,

---

[1] New impetus is given the discussion regarding Leo's sole rulership by a
study of S. P. Lambros (*Byz. Zeits. 4, 92*) based upon an inscription of the
year 895, corroborating what had already been indicated on coins, (De Saulcy,
Essai de classification des suites monetaires byzantines, 240), that Leo and
Alexander were joint sovereigns before and after the death of Basil. But
there is nothing in the Byzantine sources to warrant the opinion that they
shared the imperial power.

[2] On the matter of Leo's parentage, Zonaras (II, 166) is representative of
the leading Byzantine historians, "Basilio filius Leo ex Eudocia nascitur, qui
Michaelis esse potius credebatur, quasi praegnans fuisset Eudocia Basilio
collocata." Georg. Monach. 541, 544; Leo Grammaticus, 468, 471; Symeon
Magister, 455; Finlay, 2, 257.

[3] Below, 74.

with the judgment so long considered beyond dispute, founded
upon the study of the Basilika's drastic measures against the Jews,
and especially of those in the Novellae attributed to Leo.
Whether the men who are responsible for Ahimaaz' tradition had
any knowledge of this legislation in the Imperial Code or not,
they, as the immediate beneficiaries, positively bear witness
to a new administrative tolerance under his rule. Here the
chronicle is much more than a leisurely recital of incidents
more or less generally known. As Krauss [1] expresses it, it creates
a difficult situation. It challenges us with a new problem. And
this testimony is convincing, as has already been recognized by
authorities of the first rank.[2] It is difficult to think of it as anything but a clear statement of fact, a tradition vouched for by the
people directly affected, who would certainly know whether they
suffered the violence of persecution or were free to profess their
religion.

With this digression on the reign of Leo, which so amply
justifies itself, the author, reverting to the life of Shephatiah
under Basil, shows another phase of the stormy historical
setting of the time. He vividly describes the far-reaching
ravages of the Arabians,[3] when they overran the provinces of
Calabria and Apulia. He may not have had reference to any
particular plundering foray, but generally to the incursions
that almost incessantly made havoc in Southern Italy in the
first years of Basil's reign and earlier, as seen and experienced
by his ancestors; perhaps the general description explains
why no date is given. Nevertheless the tradition indicates the
stage of Arabian conquest in the Byzantine Empire, in which it
originated. The invaders are still in possession of Bari; it had
been taken by storm in 849, almost twenty years before the
accession of Basil; and it was used as a base from which their
frequent depredations were made, as here shown in the fall of Oria,
until it was wrested from them in 871,[4] by the combined forces of
Basil and Louis the Pious; a victory that, through a period of

[1] Krauss, *Studien 44 n. 8.*
[2] Above, *3.*
[3] Below, *74.*
[4] Finlay, *2, 249.*

lawlessness, paved the way for its ultimate submission to Byzantine administration as the supreme power in Calabria, by which the Saracens were expelled from the mainland and confined to their conquests in Sicily. The historical background is thus well preserved in the account of the life of the first generation of Amittai's descendants.

In the first half of the chronicle, almost entirely devoted to the sons of Amittai, much space is given to the general history of this period, both by the mere statement of fact and by the abundance of stories of his forefathers' experiences. There is no such profusion of historical notes in the records of the three generations immediately following. In their brief annals[1] they are barely saved from oblivion by little more than a genealogical list of the names of their representatives. However, in Paltiel, we again have a scion of the family who is favored by tradition; indeed so exceptionally favored, that his is the most conspicuous figure in the chronicle. Ahimaaz shows special satisfaction in telling the story of his remarkable career, which as Kaufmann holds,[2] may have inspired the elegy in which he is honored as the family's most illustrious son. His greatness develops in Ifrikiya and Egypt, under the patronage of the Fatimite Caliph, Abu Tamim Maad, whom the chronicle recalls only by his surname, Al Muizz. The clear record begins with his elevation to the office of vizier. The traditions tracing his rise to this eminence, such as that which tells of his first meeting with Al Muizz,[3] who was in command of an Arabian army invading Italy, who laid siege to Oria, and led the survivors of the attack into captivity, singling out and favoring Paltiel, the descendant of the great Shephatiah, evidenced a confused knowledge of this prince's life. If, as assumed, this captivity of Oria refers to that which occurred in 925, in which also the family of Donnolo[4] were taken to Sicily, the presence of Al Muizz is out of the question; he was not born until four years later (929).[5] There is no indica-

---

[1] Below, *87*.
[2] *MGWJ 40*, *538*, *552*.
[3] Below, *88*.
[4] Above, *1 note 3*.
[5] Quatremère, *Journ. As. 1836, 3s. II 29, 401*; Müller, *Der Islam, I 617*.

tion of his ever having led an expedition into Italy, either before
or after he became Caliph. The conqueror of Oria, in question,
is known to have been Jafar ibn Obaid, one of the distinguished
commanders under the father of Al Muizz.

We have no means of determining whether this confusion
appeared in the earliest traditions of Paltiel's fame, or arose
in the course of transmission. Kaufmann sees a probable explanation of it in the fact that, when these traditions were
forming, the Byzantine world resounded with the fame of
Al Muizz' amazing achievements.[1] Some substantial knowledge
of his triumphant career, extending over almost a quarter of a
century (952–976), must have been diffused among its people.
Strongholds in Sicily, that had long resisted Arabian invasion,
fell before his armies. Conquered Taormina [2] became Muizziah,
in his honor; in Southern Italy itself, his victorious armies in
command of Abul Husein were advancing and inspiring the fear
that the entire Empire, so largely exposed to attack, could not
long defend itself against them. At the zenith of his power, he
was the acknowledged and dreaded organizer of brilliant victory.
In minds that could not but be engrossed in this dominant
personality among the sovereigns known to them, there was little
room for the thought of the less imposing figures who carried
his plans of conquest into execution, and were the actual commanders of his armies. This vivid impression might easily have
led to such popular belief as the chronicle expresses in mis-
taking him for the commander of the Arabian armies in Italy.
This initial mistake, however, must not be taken as an index
to the value of all that is contained in this story of Paltiel.
There is sufficient accuracy of detail to offset it. At the very
outset, there is a true appreciation of one of the conspicuous
traits of Al Muizz, his absorbing interest in astrology and
fondness for its adepts.[3] It is as a master of astrology that
Paltiel is first befriended by him. Again the development of
his power is in the main correctly traced; from the submission

[1] *MGWJ 40, 530.*
[2] Quatremère, *Journ. As., 1837, 64.*
[3] Quatremère, *1837, 207.*

of Sicily, the first great acquisition of his reign, to the culminating conquest of Egypt, six years before his death.

While the chronicle is in error in naming the conquest of Ifrikiya one of his achievements, as though Fatimite power had not already been established there, with its seat of authority at Kairowan,[1] it shows at least logical adherence to its own point of view, that begins by simply declaring that the Caliph was in Italy, makes no attempt to go back of that fact, and seems to imply that the encampment there was the center of authority from which the creation of his domain proceeded. The emissaries of Sicily, as the nearest suppliants, would naturally be the first to appeal to him there. Having established his power in Sicily, a new task calls him to Ifrikiya, that proffers its allegiance to him. And here, finally, the envoys of Egypt implore him to extend his triumphant sovereignty over their country. Upon its fundamental assumption, the story of conquest is consistently told. The statements that are clearly unhistorical are confined to the false assumption of Al Muizz' presence at the conquest of Oria; of his rule, in person, over Sicily, and the confused enumeration of his chief conquests. We almost lose sight of these errors, in the many details, in which there is complete agreement with the accounts of the Arabian and Byzantine historians. The expedition into Egypt is minutely described, although there is no mention of the years devoted to the preparation[2] for it, corresponding practically word for word to what is accepted as the historical account of it. The omission of the evidence of opposition to the army of occupation, does not seriously mar its perception of the fact that this conquest was actually a bloodless one; a fact upon which all sources are agreed, counting the short-lived hostility of the Ikshid partisans,[3] of too little weight to be regarded as an appreciable interference with the peaceful investment of the country. Again, no fault can be found as to the accuracy of detail in the account of the Byzantine Embassy that sought audience with the Caliph. The author is

[1] Muir, The Caliphate (1915), 558.
[2] Quatremère, 1836, 423; Lane-Poole, Egypt in the Middle Ages, 101.
[3] DeGoeje, ZDMG 52, 75; Quatremère, Journ. As. ibid.

manifestly at great pains to do justice to this chapter in his famous ancestor's life, to linger upon the lavishly magnificent setting of the royal court in which he commands. The amazing, artistic completeness has no trace of disordered and fragmentary tradition. It shows a thorough familarity with what we already know of the elaborate ceremonialism of such Byzantine missions, and of the splendor of the Fatimite court, a splendor heretofore unknown in that fertile strip of country between Mauretania and Egypt, by the extraordinary display of which, as described in the chronicle, the Macedonian ambassador was to be impressed with the incomparable wealth of the caliph. We cannot but note how closely it follows the stories that have come down to us, of such imperial missions sent from time to time to establish relations of amity between the Byzantine Empire and the Caliphate.

In the days of Theophilos, in the year 833, the renowned John the Grammarian was sent to enter into diplomatic negotiations with Motassem. In this instance it was the representative of Byzantine opulence that amazed the Arabians with the display of rare treasures; by his assumed indifference to the disappearance of a costly ewer and basin, which he had shrewdly planned with the help of his attendants, and by other devices calculated to add to the wonder of the Saracens at the wealth of the Christians. Later, Zoe, the widow of Leo VI., Empress Regent during the minority of Constantine Porphyrogenitus, sought an alliance with Moktader through a similar embassy, the account of which gives particulars of the luxurious ceremonialism of the occasion, that are, almost to the letter, like those of the anecdote in the chronicle, excepting that it does not include the incident of the Ambassador's refusal to be presented to the Caliph by a Jewish Master of the palace, and of his eventual acceptance of the situation, in the confession of his unworthy malice and arrogance. In all probability, however, all such records are modelled after the story of the remarkable embassy by which this same Constantine, as Emperor, sought the friendship of Abd-al-Rahman III. (912–961), that was remembered above all others seen in the streets of his capital, to do homage to the ruler whose "fame penetrated the most remote and barbarous regions of the globe."

The traditions of Ahimaaz are more comprehensive than any of these. They contain both the allusion to the device of the precious ewer and basin that is especially recalled in the one, and the priceless trappings and extravagant pleasures of the Saracen Court, that are emphasized in the other; and, as far as the latter is concerned, it bears upon an event that occurred in the time of Paltiel. In this passage, then, we may have the earliest Hebrew version of a popular tradition, that, nearly three centuries after the chronicle had been written, was still thought worthy of lengthy repetition in Abulfeda's "Abridgment of the History of Mankind" (1328). The sameness of vivid detail in such stories of diplomatic intercourse, varying only in the assignment of surpassing display, now to the Emperor and now to the Caliph, must have contributed to their diffusion and retention among the people,

The commanding figure that advises and rules as vizier of Al Muizz is, in this Jewish tradition, Paltiel, of whom there is no mention in any other chronicle. In view of the general reliability of the chronicle regarding the life of this caliph, we cannot deny this strange hero a substantial claim upon our attention. We must consider the position of Kaufmann[1] well taken; when discussing the importance of this part of the chronicle, as a contribution to the history of Fatimite Egypt, he holds that there must be historical foundation for this tradition. In the opinion of DeGoeje,[2] likewise, there can be no doubt that it has a basis of truth. He meets the difficulty by declaring that we must choose between discarding it as fictitious and worthless, or receiving it upon the assumption that Paltiel does appear in the histories, but under another name. Adopting the latter theory, he points out how very closely the account of Ahimaaz follows all that is said of the chief counsellor and most distinguished general of Al Muizz, Jauhar, a captive from Southern Italy, variously named in Arabian histories, the Roman, the Slav, the

---

[1] *MGWJ 40, 540; ZDMG 51, 436 ff.*

[2] *ZDMG, 52, 75, 79.* Bacher, *REJ 32, 148,* "Après tous les émondages nécessaires, il en reste encore assez pour que la situation de Paltiel paraisse comme extraordinairement éminente." Poznanski, *REJ 48, 145,* finds in the story of Paltiel "un noyau historique."

Sicilian, and always surnamed Al Katib, which is probably suggestive of his original position as secretary to Mansur, Al Muizz' father. DeGoeje disposes of this well-known name by regarding it as nothing more than a surname, given by Al Muizz, in accordance with a custom of the day, by which favorite slaves were distinguished as Lu'lu (pearl), Jauhar (jewel), Yaqut (ruby), upon being converted to Islam. Kaufmann had also, but less confidently, inclined to a similar theory when he saw this ancestor of Ahimaaz hidden in the name of Ibn Killis,[1] the Bagdad apostate, who, having been driven from eminent service under the Ikshid sovereign Kafur (966), by his vizier's intrigues, won the favor of Al Muizz, and of his son Al Aziz, under whom he served as vizier for fifteen years.

But the theory as applied by these authorities has a serious weakness, as DeGoeje[2] admits, in that it takes no account of the hero's loyalty to Judaism. Between a Jauhar,[3] whose adoption of Mohammedanism is beyond question and an Ibn Killis,[4] about whose apostasy there is equal certainty, and a Paltiel who, amid all the rewards of his high station is conspicuously true to his ancestral faith, there is no resemblance. This theory takes us too far afield and gives no promise of penetrating the mystery. The strict adherence to the text may suggest a solution. As a master of astrology,[5] in which capacity he strongly appealed to Al Muizz, he may have been the caliph's specially trusted adviser, a sort of power behind the throne, not generally counted among the officials in power, but through his confidential relations with the caliph, actually determining adminstrative policy, planning campaigns of conquest, practically serving as vizier. Further supporting the plausibility of Ahimaaz' story, is the fact that Al Muizz was a remarkably liberal and tolerant sovereign, ranking high as a prince zealous for justice and devoted to learning, to which the chronicle bears witness with its eminent case in point, as it does also to the same spirit of broad-minded

[1] Kaufmann, *MGWJ 40, 536.*
[2] DeGoeje *ZDMG 52, 80.*
[3] Quatremère, *Journ. As., 1837, 44.*
[4] Quatremère, *Journ. As., 1837, 186.*
[5] Below, *89.*

administration in Al Aziz, his son and successor; nor does it over-look the shadow of the picture, the bitter animosity[1] of the native officials against the Jewish court favorite. With Paltiel, the slanders fail of their purpose.[2] The favor and affection of the Caliph are intensified; the conspirators are overwhelmed with shame. The fate of this favorite is not like that of others chosen by Al Aziz,[3] a Jewish vizier in Syria and a Christian in Eygpt, in defense of whom he almost lost his life, and whom popular clamor and intolerance finally compelled him to remove in disgrace.

While Kaufmann and DeGoeje agree that, in the main, the chronicle tells a story remarkably free from historical inaccuracy, they are certain that its concluding anecdote[4] is altogether misplaced; that the prediction, read in the suddenly vanishing stars, of the death, in rapid succession within the year, of three kings, must have been made to Al Muizz and not to his son. DeGoeje holds that only by that assumption can the astrologer's vision be made to include not only the death of the three kings, but also that of Al Muizz and Paltiel, all of whom died within the year in question. We may, however, question, with Kaufmann, whether the message of the stars was made to include Al Muizz still in power and the astrologer himself. Post eventum knowledge of all these details may be responsible for the opinion of these authorities. If we follow the tradition of the chronicle that Al Muizz,[5] some time before his death, called his son to the throne, implying that he lived long enough to see the continuance of his family's power at the hands of his successor, guided by the coun-sel of Paltiel, there is no error in ascribing this event to the time of Al Aziz, even though it might be necessary to ascribe it to the first year of his reign. Moreover, reading into the interpretation of the astrologer, the exact knowledge of history acquired through subsequent study is not warranted in the light of the

---

[1] Kremer, *Culturgeschichte, I, 188;* Lane Poole, *Egypt in the M. A., 120;* Below, *95.*

[2] Below, *96.*

[3] Lane-Poole, *Egypt in the M. A., 120.*

[4] Kaufmann, *ZDMG 51, 442.*

[5] Below, *95.* Quatremère, *Journ. As., 1837, 202.*

usual vagueness of oracles and similar revelations of the future.
The year 976 proved to be the fateful year. In rapid succession,
beginning with the death of Al Muizz at the close of 975, there
occurred the death of John,[1] Emperor of Byzantium, who, returning from an expedition to the East, was poisoned by conspirators; of Al Hakam, the Caliph of the West; of Rokn, the
Caliph of Bagdad, and of Paltiel.

As we reach the end of the story in the impassioned tribute to
the man whom the great Caliph had so signally honored, in the
survey of his far-reaching jurisdiction over the provinces of the
Caliphate, in the recollection of his worthy preeminence as
Nagid[2] of the Jews of the country, we are the more convinced
that this brilliant career is not the creation of irresponsible
fancy. Conceding that Ahimaaz as a man of letters with some
knowledge of the current descriptions of the glories of Arabian power almost a century before his time, availed himself
of apposite records that would supplement his fragmentary
annals, incorporating what was amply warranted by the shattered
testimony regarding the exceptional eminence of Paltiel, we do
not thereby impair his chronicle's value as a source of sound information. It would still seem true that there was enough family
tradition to make possible just such elaboration, not at all out
of porportion to the real distinction of the great ancestor. That
Ahimaaz will not be bound by the severe restrictions of the
crude annalist is more evident here than in any other section
of the chronicle, when he further dwells upon this happy memory
in a noteworthy elegy.[3]

Following closely upon this life-story of Paltiel, is the account
of another renowned scion of the family, Samuel, a cousin[4] of
Paltiel, who flourished at the close of the tenth century, in
Capua, as the minister of finance, with supervision over all departments of government under the Lombard princes of that
duchy. In the latter, the setting is naturally less brilliant than
that of the former, and the story is much more briefly told, but

[1] Finlay, *2, 360*.
[2] Poznanski, *REJ 48, 144*; Below, *99*.
[3] Below, *97*.
[4] Below, *97*.

it shows the same accurate knowledge of its locale.   Here again
the chronicle brings to light a man of whom we have had no knowledge, but there is an additional reason for accepting what is
said of him.   The obscurity from which the earlier traditions had
to be extricated could not, to the same extent, have prevailed in
the recollections of the life of the author's own grandfather.
For these facts there was no long and perilous line of transmission.
They were gathered from the vivid memories of those who could
testify as eye witnesses, his father and the elders of the community
of Capua in which he had spent his youth.   And before leaving
his birthplace for Oria, he himself surely saw the thriving life to
which the Jews attained there; so that this tradition of the
chronicle is, in part, a glowing description of his personal
experience.   We are therefore constrained to add the name of
Samuel b. Hananeel to the list of the illustrious Jews whose
service to the state brought them the favor of princes.

If this work of Ahimaaz has real value for the biographical
notes in which it abounds, and for the historical episodes relating
to great men and events in a vital chapter of Byzantine history,
and in the resplendent era of Fatimite ascendancy, it serves
equally well, both with its explicit and its implied information,
to set forth the social and political conditions under which the
Jews lived in Southern Italy and neighboring sections of the
Byzantine Empire during the two centuries of the rise and fall
of the Basilian dynasty.   Amittai and his sons are men of learning
and of letters, masters of public instruction, and, at the same
time, students of secret wisdom and adepts in its use.   Likewise
their contemporary, Abu Aaron, is remembered for his power to
triumph over and exorcise evil spirits, but also, and at greater
length, for his vast knowledge of Talmudic Law, and his wise
application of it, for the inspiration of his example in his ardent
encouragement of the schools.   This double view-point is typical
of the traditions of the chronicle, and controls Ahimaaz himself.
Even in the case of Paltiel, whose life was so largely that of a man
of affairs, attention is divided between the mystic and astrologer
and the practical administrator, embodied in the same character.
It reveals now a yielding to superstition and now a vigorous as-

sertion of intelligence. Occasionally, as was true of Hai Gaon[1], an exceptional mind rises sufficiently above this theory and practice of mysticism, to denounce it for what it is. The one-sided judgment passed upon the intellectual activity of these mediaeval Jewish communities, is born of the exclusive consideration of their weakness for superstition, and takes no account of the strength that also manifests itself in defense of true learning and intelligent living. There is a strong temptation to hold to it upon the ground that, according to the popular verdict, all things Byzantine are barbarous,[2] and that the stream of Jewish life in that mediaeval world could not have risen higher than its source. But to insist upon it is to ignore the evidence that proves such an assumption false.

The depravity frequently conspicuous in Byzantine life, led Graetz[3] to believe that the same conditions must have prevailed among the Jews who were a part of it, and that therefore nothing noteworthy could have been produced by them; that in the foulness of their environment, they could at best have developed nothing more than mediocre ability as sluggish pupils of foreign masters of learning; that, accordingly, their sages were the butt of the ridicule of the sages of the Babylonian Academies.[4] In his opinion, the period between Shabbethai Donnolo and the author of Tana debe Eliahu could not have been anything but a void, unrelieved by any Jewish literary or intellectual effort of particular value. As he knew of no work comparable to the Tachkemoni,[5] that, in these two centuries, might seem to have been inspired by it, he believed that all possible evidence had been obtained, and concluded that this was a dismal period of mental stagnation. This is indeed an extreme use of the argumentum e silentio. Güdemann,[6] less arbitrarily, reaches substantially the same conclusion as to the feeble intellectual striving of the Jews of the Byzantine Empire. In his analysis

[1] Graetz, *6, 4.*

[2] Gelzer, *Byz. Kulturgesch, 2 ff.*; C. Neumann, *Die Weltstellung d. byz. Reiches vor d. Kruezzügen, 18;* Freeman, *Historical Essays, III, 231 ff.*

[3] Graetz, *5, 315.*

[4] Graetz, *5, 318.*

[5] Above, *3.*

[6] *Gesch. II, 55.*

of the Tana debe Eliahu, in which he sees the indications of the end of the crude, first period of Jewish history in Italy, and of the beginning of an age of scientific activity, he assigns to the Italian communities a place between those of Spain and France, to explain the contrast that he finds between their respective stages of culture. Whereas the Jews of Spain were stimulated by the culture of the Arabians; and those of France, through their isolation on account of difficulty of communication with the Orient, thrust upon their own resources, determined to give all possible attention to the preservation of their traditions, the Jews of Italy were not influenced by either of these forces. Amid general degradation, they had no incentive to culture; besides they were not familiar enough with Arabic, to make use of its literature. And as they were not isolated from Babylon and Africa, the great sources of Jewish learning, they simply depended upon them, confining themselves to an insignificant study of the Talmud.

This opinion of conditions as they were in Italy in the eleventh century when, as Güdemann says, a day of enlightenment was beginning to dawn, would probably have seemed to him to apply with greater force to the earlier centuries that, in his judgment, were not enlivened by the demands of the awakening mind. As far as Jewish life in the Byzantine Empire is concerned there is no recognition, in these opinions, of its claim to more than passing notice. The method of study is obviously at fault that makes what is known of Rome and the West serve as the basis of generalization about the conditions in the Empire of the East, loosely judging the one by the other, as though Rome were still the chief seat of power, and Byzantine sovereignty, centered in Constantinople, negligible. The fact is that the life emanating from this new capital had very little in common with that which looked to Rome; the former capital had rapidly yielded supremacy to the new center of authority, that realized the ambition of Constantine, its founder; that developed its own history of more than a thousand years. It is a far cry from opinions so crudely determined to that of Zunz,[1] who attributes the preservation of the traditions of Jewish learning in Italy, as in other lands, when

[1] *GV 323, 373ff.*

the schools of the Geonim were closed in 1040,[1] to the fact that for centuries the Jews of Italy under Byzantine rule had thoroughly prepared themselves for such a task; and to that of Krauss and Eppenstein, among more recent authorities, who prove that the Byzantine period of Jewish history can no longer be decried as a time of notorious degradation and intellectual poverty. It is the more trustworthy judgment, resting upon the discoveries of half a century, unknown to the earlier students, documents that have given new impetus to the study of this chapter of imperial history, that have compelled the revision of our interpretation of its life. In addition to the aid of the new sources [2] bearing upon the general history of the Byzantine Empire, later scholars have had the testimony of the chronicle of Ahimaaz, which has been further supported by the "Hoard of Hebrew Manuscripts"[3] almost simultaneously unearthed by Schechter in the Geniza of the old Synagog at Fostat, near Cairo. The information gained from them easily leads us to believe, with Krauss[4] that "the influence of the Byzantine Jews on Judaism in general is much greater than has heretofore been acknowledged." It is now more evident that there was in Byzantine life not only naïve reveling in the supernatural but also rational yearning for and cultivation of knowledge.

This is true especially of the period through which Ahimaaz traces his lineage, from the time that the strong hand of Basil I. arrested the decline of the Empire, and replaced fatalistic corruption with vigorous aspiration. Superstition looms large in the story but it does not crowd out the interest in higher pursuits. Emperor and people had frequent recourse to the arts of the astrologer and the representatives of secret wisdom, but they also encouraged the study of medicine, philosophy, grammar and jurisprudence. Amid the vicissitudes of the two centuries of Basilian rule, education was at no time utterly abandoned. It is true that schools were not always maintained

---

[1] Graetz, *5, 345ff.*

[2] Below, *58*.

[3] Adler, *Jews in many Lands, 145;* Ginzberg, *Geonica I, IX.* Schechter, *Studies in Judaism,* II, *1-30.*

[4] Krauss, *Byzantine Empire, JE III, 450.*

with equal ardor. They had their days of conspicuous glory; and, under stress of tumult, they languished. The conditions may be understood as incident to an age of transition, in which a growing spirit of intelligence was contending with deeply intrenched powers of darkness. Photius, the man of learning, the gifted and prolific writer, the eminent teacher surrounded by students from all parts of the world, in his writings, mingling stories of the miraculous with discourses on the principles of philosophy, is representative of the intellectual struggle among the people of his day. There must have been enough popular interest in teachers and schools to make such a master possible. Between this towering figure at the beginning of the period under consideration and that of the "Prince of Philosophers," Psellus, at its close, there always were teachers, giving instruction in private and public schools. The studies of Giesebrecht, continuing the labors of Muratori and Tiraboschi, establish this fact beyond question. His conclusion, bearing upon educational activity in the Byzantine Empire as far back as the eighth century, is "Ex eo tempore non in majoribus modo urbibus, sed et in villis vicisque scholae publicae erant in quibus primis quidem litterarum elementis pueri erudiebantur; neque minus certum est, eodem tempore inter Longobardos doctores exstitisse qui grammatici vocantur, artibus liberalibus pro temporum illorum conditione non mediocriter instructos."[1] It implies simply the fair reading of such contemporaneous testimony as that of Gerbert, who, in a visit to Italy at the end of the tenth century, is impressed with the country as a field for the purchase of books; and that of Wipo, the chaplain of Conrad II., who laments Germany's marked intellectual inferiority to Italy where "the entire youth is sent to sweat in the schools."

The investigations[2] of our own day have but emphasized the

[1] Giesebrecht, De litterarum studiis apud Italos primis medii aevi saeculis, 7, 8; Ozanam, Documents inédits pour servir à l'histoire littéraire de l'Italie depuis 8 au 13 siecle, 5–13; Balzani, Early Chroniclers of Italy, 181; Wattenbach, Deutschlands Quellengeschichte im Mittelalter, 7 Ed., 307, 347; Taylor, The Mediaeval Mind, 248; Bikélas, La Grèce Byzantine et Moderne, 69 ff; Gothein, Die Culturentwickelung Süd-Italiens, 2 ff.

[2] Taylor, The Med. Mind, 248.

fact that in Byzantium, "there was always some demand for instruction in Grammar and Law; that there never ceased to be schools conducted by laymen for laymen, where instruction in matters profane and secular was imparted." Freeman[1] has not overshot the mark in saying that profound scholars and acute theologians were the natural product of the soil. The schools were in an especially flourishing condition under Constantine VII. The universities at Constantinople and at Salerno[2] were widely known centers of learning. This stimulation of scholarly activity gave distinction to an entire century, of which Krumbacher[3] says: "Auf das Zeitalter des Photius folgt das weniger durch originelle Erzeugnisse als durch grossartige Sammelthätigkeit hervorragende zehnte Jahrhundert, das man als das Jahrhundert der Enzyklopädien bezeichnen könnte." Granted that the learned men of Byzantium, in possession of the treasures of classical antiquity, generally showed but little individuality in presenting them, mostly confining themselves to collections of extracts, to notes and summaries; these compilations, by their number and by their literary merit, point to the existence of a public that, to such appreciable extent, encouraged intellectual life—the people of an Empire whose capital, "in the history of mediaeval civilization before the eleventh century, played a rôle analogous to that of Athens and Rome in antiquity, its influence extending over the whole world, pre-eminently *the* city."[4] This was especially true in the tenth century, the "Golden Age of Byzantine history." Under its centralized depotism that,[5] "in an age when order and freedom were irreconcilable, was positively the best government in the world, life and property were most secure; art, literature, commerce and general civilization, flourishing." In the judgment of Sandys,[6] "of the extant remains of Byzantine Literature, apart

---

[1] Freeman, *Historical Essays III*, 236.

[2] "To the Jews is largely due the building up of the school of Salerno which we find flourishing in the 10th century," White, *Warfare of Science with Theology, II, 33;* Abrahams, *Jewish Life in Middle Ages, XIX;* Bédarride, *Les Juifs en France, etc., 106.*

[3] Krumbacher, *Gesch. d. byz. Lit.*, 16.

[4] Munro and Sellery, *Mediaeval Civilization, 212, 223.*

[5] Freeman, Historical Essays, III, 274.

[6] Sandys, *I, 424.*

from theological works, nearly half belong to the domain of scholarship in the widest sense of the term." The popular intel igence that demanded schools and teachers, also manifested itself in other practical directions. In Sicily, it was quick to recognize the more equitable system of taxation of the Arabian conquerors, as contrasted with the extortionate policy of the emperors. Again, it boldly protested against the notorious and defiant shamelessness of the Emperor Constantine VI. and prevailed against him.

In addition to the impulses from within to promote culture, vitalized by the contemplation of the classic heritage, there were powerful influences from without, that disputed the field with barbarism in the Byzantine Empire. The Arabian conquests upon its soil became so many points of direct contact with the astounding civilization of the Caliphate. Furthermore, the Empire lay in the very path of this triumphant power and irresistible culture,[1] whether the approach was from the East or from the West. It surely could not have prevented the penetration of such forces. Cultural isolation from the not very distant Ommeyyad domain in Spain, would have been as difficult as a geographical one. If the emperors had in mind only the political advantage to be gained by an alliance with such dominant power, the effects of the friendly relations could not actually have been so restricted. An embassy like that of Constantine Porphyrogenitus to Abd-er-Rahman III., would result in much more than an assurance of the great Caliph's favor. The envoys' impressions of the glories of Cordova must have contributed materially to its fame in Byzantium. The city that, especially under Al Hakem II., the renowned patron of letters, was the foremost meeting place of the world's students and writers, must have roused to emulation also its Byzantine visitors and students, by the instruction of its schools and libraries, by the tangible evidences of its administration, in the productive fields, in its well-drained and lighted streets.

In this society, "the study of letters had become the popular

[1] Scott, *Moor. Emp. in Europe, I 34.*

and absorbing pursuit."[1]   Furthermore, when Alexandria was no
longer open to the commerce of the western Caliphate, its subjects
were amply indemnified by the hospitable reception which they
habitually received from the people of Constantinople.   "It
was a judicious and enlightened policy,[2] and one whose important influence on every branch of art and learning cannot be
estimated by the material prosperity, however great, which its
institution conferred, that dictated the alliance, and preserved
the close relations long existing between the princes of Moorish
Spain and the sovereigns of Byzantium."   The outstanding feature
of Arabian progress among mediaeval nations, was the intellectual
impetus which it gave.   The predatory hordes "effected a great
intellectual revolution in every country which submitted to their
sway.   By precept and example they aroused the emulation and
rewarded the efforts of all who struggled to escape from the
fetters of ignorance which had been riveted by the superstition
and prejudice of ages passed in ignominious servitude."[3]   We
cannot assume that such effects of their invasion were unknown in the Eastern Empire alone.   In Southern Italy where
there was direct contact with Greeks and Arabs, there must
have been a decided penetration of the fertilizing influence of
their respective civilizations.[4]   They may have been advanced
both by eager acceptance and by unconscious assimilation.
Granted that there was more of the latter than of the former,
the result was none the less real and noteworthy.

As a part of the population of the Empire, the Jews must be
similarly judged.   Where forces of education were at work, they
could not have given all their strength to the inanities of superstition.   All that we know of Jewish life under similar
conditions warrants the belief that in this instance also, they ardently seized the opportunities for intellectual exertion.   This
general observation now has something more than probability
to commend it.   The severe verdict of Güdemann on the Jews
of Mediaeval Italy seems to have been less firmly spoken by him

[1] Scott, *I, 671.*
[2] Scott, *I, 176.*
[3] Scott, *I, 14.*
[4] Balzani, *Early Chroniclers . . ., 181.*

than that in which he assigns to them preeminence among those
who made of Italy the great entrepôt of the literary treasures
of the Orient, as it was of the commerce between the East and
the West. There is no trace of faint praise in the words, "Durch
das ganze Mittelalter hindurch, das man ja längst aufgehört hat
als eine Zeit der Stagnation zu betrachten, zeigt sich eine stetige,
dem allgemeinen Culturfortschritte parallellaufende Fortbewe-
gung unter den Italienischen Juden, durch welche sie vorber-
eitet werden, um in die neuere Zeit als die ersten unter ihren
europäischen Glaubensgenossen mit Verständniss and Begeist-
erung einzugehen."[1] More comprehensive but equally positive
is the statement of the leading authority on Byzantine-Jewish
studies of the present day, "In keinem Lande Europas, auch in
Spanien und Italien nicht, waren die Juden so innig mit der
Sprache und Kultur ihres Heimatlandes verwachsen als in
Byzanz—Kein Land in Europa hat in der Sprache, in der Poesie,
in der Liturgie, in den rabbinisch-religiösen Schriften der Juden
solch tiefe Spuren zurückgelassen als das mittelalterliche Byzanz."[2] Greek Jews, especially from Constantinople, frequently
visited the academies of Babylon. Hai Gaon was indebted to
them for his knowledge of Greek.

In the light of the traditions of Ahimaaz, this view is the
only defensible one. As a whole, the family record is the story
of a succession of sages and masters of instruction, eminent
men of letters during the eventful Basilian period. As such
it leaves no doubt as to the cultural status of the communities
that encourage and honor these masters. The visit[3] of a sage
evokes their fervid hospitality. There is a general appreciation
of his ancestors' liturgical poetry. From the schools of Oria[4]
their native city, the chief seat of learning, the light radiates
into the neighboring communities. The lapse[5] from the high
standard of learning and reverence is lamented as a fatal offense.
It is a story of thriving communities; there is no suggestion of

[1] Güdemann, *II*, *7*.
[2] Krauss, *Studien*, *99*.
[3] Below, *64*.
[4] Below, *66*.
[5] Below, *87*.

difficulties of communication between one city and another,
between them and the capital, or between one country and another.
Abu Aaron is not hindered in his travels from his home in Bagdad.
Wayfaring[1] and pilgrimages are mentioned as of common oc-
currence, with nothing to interfere with them, except the danger
to the caravans of being plundered. Furthermore, the conditions
of life reflect varying influences as the cities are ruled in turn
by Lombard prince, Byzantine emperor, or Arabian conqueror.
The author himself, writing his chronicle as the Basilian dynasty
comes to an end, shows, in the highly developed form of his work,
the literary acumen resulting from contact with at least three
influences, that of Jewish tradition, of Byzantine literary practice
(acrostic hymn), and of the Arabian (rimed prose). The
expressed desire of Ahimaaz to give an intelligible account of his
ancestry, justifies the inference that, in his choice of this form of
narrative, he was guided by the preference of the poeple for
whom he wrote. He may, both for the form and the matter of
his work, be regarded as representative of Jewish communal
life that had had sufficient intellectual discipline, to value the
memory of its sages and poets so highly.

The chronicle is an important document not only for its
direct evidence relating to the family of Amittai. The lines of
the story are admittedly limited in scope, confined to the experiences of one family, whose activities were mostly devoted
to school and synagog. Paltiel, the great counsellor of Al Muizz
and his son, and Samuel, the minister of finance in Capua, are
the exceptions to the rule. But its indirect evidence for the
general social and political milieu, is equally important.
The larger story is easily read between the lines. Even if the
traditions did not actually describe noteworthy communal
prosperity, made possible in a measure through the distinguished
service of a Paltiel, or Samuel, they cannot be understood as
records of experience wholly detached and different from that of
the mass of the people. The very existence of the schools in
which these men taught, and of the literature they produced
during eight generations, is conditioned by a social order

[1] Below, 65. Abrahams, *Book of Delight, 122.*

essentially free from privation and oppression; in which alone
the yearning for higher mental and spiritual nourishment can so
freely express itself. A more comprehensive account of the life
of which these men were a part would undoubtedly have had
much to say of its material phase, of the commercial and other
occupations of the workaday world in which the sustenance of
their culture was obtained. The general experience epitomized
in this Jewish document distinctly reflects the favorable conditions
in the Byzantine Empire that made it possible. Upon its
authority we have the more reason to believe that there were
strong liberalizing forces at work, effecting a substantial measure
of freedom throughout the land.

It is generally believed that Italy,[1] throughout its history, holds
an exceptional place among the nations of Europe for its tolerance
towards the Jews. The especially favored explanation of it is,
that the country was divided into many principalities, later
republics, their energies all bent upon destroying one another.
Güdemann's clear statement of it leaves the impression that,
until the fifteenth century, such anarchic conditions weakened
the strong arm of government that might otherwise have exerted
itself in persecution. It does not even hint at the existence of
the centralized Byzantine administration that, for centuries,
prevailed in Longobardia, the territory of the rival princes. It
is under this very power that the family of Ahimaaz lives most of
its life. But to distinguish politically and historically between
Lombard and Byzantine Italy, is not to deny the substantial
accuracy of the estimate of the country's preeminence. The
chronicle of Ahimaaz bears witness to it. What is said by
Abrahams,[2] of Italy "as the scene in all ages of close literary
friendships between Jews and Christians such as no other country could show in the same profusion," he verifies by an instance
from this very period of its history, the friendship between Donnolo and Saint Nilus.

The spirit of that generation could not have languished as
Byzantine civilization advanced in its Golden Age. The view,

[1] Depping, *Les Juifs dans le Moyen Age, 101.*
[2] Abrahams, *Jewish Life in the M. A., 419.*

at close range, that the chronicle gives of Jewish literary activity
in the Byzantine Empire, discloses much more than halting
receivers of the learning of the Geonim. There is original
and independent effort in the devotion to and the elaboration
of the Piyyut.[1] That the Byzantine Jews gloried in this contribution to our Literature, Ahimaaz plainly records as he tells of the
days to which we assign its vigorous growth. Shall we ignore
their estimate of this distinctively Byzantine Jewish product?
Is it a weak link in the chain of Jewish literary tradition? The
prolific labors of Jannai and Kalir, of their colleagues and successors, affected Jewish life far beyond their own time and country.
The liturgical poem is not the only claim of these mediaeval
communities to special consideration. There is originality also
in their promulgation of the usual learning of the central
academies in Babylon and in Palestine; a characteristic freedom
of discourse and exposition in public instruction, is justly attributed to them. But, whereas this manifestation of independent
intellect is not to be overlooked, it is less noteworthy than its
very vigorous expression in the abundance of the sacred poetry of
the synagog. Original productivity along the more familiar
traditional lines of Jewish learning cannot be the only test of
eminent cultural achievement. There was an insistent demand
for it also in the development of the synagog's liturgy. We
cannot with reason think of this contribution as a wide and senseless departure from Jewish tradition. Issuing from Palestine,
where the more emotional appeal of the Haggada had inspired
the pioneers in this form of literature, it grew to maturity
upon Byzantine soil. Its spiritual appeal was probably the
determining factor responsible for its ardent cultivation at the
hands of the Jews of that country.

The inclination to cherish such an inheritance would be
especially strong where the atmosphere was charged with
encouragement of it, as it was when the liturgy of the dominant
Byzantine church was so elaborately developed. Here it
set its own standards with astounding freedom, and became a
unique embodiment of intellectual and spiritual vigor. As a

[1] Above, 6; Berliner II, 15.

contribution to Jewish Liturgy, both in quantity and quality it cannot be negligible. That the liturgy of the synagog has been a vitalizing factor of signal importance in Jewish life, is beyond question. Emphasizing this fact, L. Ginzberg[1] protests against the misunderstanding of the importance of the activities of the Geonim, for this cogent reason among others, that "upon no other department has their influence been more important than upon the Liturgy." To do justice to the labors of the Paitanim, we should accept the conclusion of Eppenstein in his study of the history and literature of the Geonic Age,[2] "Wenn die Palästinenser auch nicht die Geistesschärfe der Babylonier in dem Lehrverhandlungen hervortreten liessen, so haben sie dafür aus der Tiefe ihres Gemütes die schönen Perlen der vielgestaltigen Gebete emporgeholt." Ahimaaz is our trustworthy guide through this domain of the poetic soul reveling in the latitude of artistic and didactic fantasy; an illumined soul that would demand zeal for the traditions of learning and piety, that alone would account for such a chapter of intellectual progress as Zunz finds, from the emergence of the Byzantine Jews from obscurity in the eighth century to the time of flourishing study in the tenth, when the sages of Bari were the peers of the Geonim. In the opinion of Eppenstein, the dictum of Graetz:[3] "Überhaupt haben die italienischen Juden in keinem Fache Meisterschaft erlangt; sie blieben stets fleissige Jünger fremder Lehrer. In Babylonien machte man sich daher über die Weisen Roms," d. h. Italiens, weidlich lustig," must be abandoned for, "die Gegenteilige Schilderung in der Chronik des Achimaaz von Oria."

Again the memoirs of Ahimaaz are almost entirely free from evidences of active antagonism on the part of the people or the government. They indeed have their records of sorrow. The Jews during these two centuries naturally did not escape the visitations that frequently convulsed the land. Pestilence, captivity at the hands of the invader, disaster through political upheaval; but, in the main, there is nothing to indicate that they suffered as the victims of a sustained policy of repression.

[1] *Geonica I, VIII.*
[2] *MGWJ 52.*
[3] Graetz, *5, 332 n.*

The reign of Basil I. is vividly remembered as the only time in which they had such sorrow. In its sadness it stands out in the record. It is always designated as *the* persecution. This tradition bears out the view that mediaeval Italy was conspicuous for its liberal treatment of the Jews. The fact that the historians of the day seldom single them out for mention and that in the code of the Lombards [1] no special legislation refers to them, may well prove as Berliner argues, that there was no general persecution of them. The difficulties of government in the midst of endless clashes between principalities, or between ecclesiastical factions, each seeking its own gain, while the way was thereby opened to the plundering invaders, may have crowded out all thought of harassing the Jews. From the beginning of the sixth century when the Lombard princes rose to power, their internecine wars were almost incessant. Italy therefore became "une foule de petits états plus occupés à se guerroyer les uns les autres qu'à régler les droits de leurs sujets." [2] In this state of political chaos there may have been respite for the Jews. The conditions are aptly summarized by Reinach, [3] "Les Lombards qui succédèrent aux Grecs dans le nord de l'Italie traitèrent les Juifs avec douceur; il faut venir jusqu'au carolingien Louis II. pour trouver un édit d'expulsion (885) inspiré par le clergé et qui ne fut pas d'ailleurs exécuté. Bientôt d'ailleurs, le morcellement politique de la péninsule les ravages des Arabes et des Normands, la lutte de la papauté et de l'empire allemand détournèrent des Juifs l'attention des gouvernements et du clergè et leur permirent de vivre cachés, c'est-à-dire assez heureux."

But we cannot accept this negative explanation as adequate. There must have been a more substantial basis for this undeniable freedom. It is more probably due to the position which the

---

[1] Berliner, II 6: "als die anfangs noch arianische Longobarden in Italien eindrangen, wurde das Recht der Longobarden eingeführt in welchem zwar der Juden selbst nicht erwähnt wird, aus welchem Umstande aber gefolgert werden darf, dass jede Ausnahmestellung für sie wegfiel."

Dresdner, *Kultur und Sittengeschichte der Italienischen Geistlichkeit im 10 und 11 Jahrhundert (1890), 16.*

[2] Bédarride, *62ff.*

[3] Histoire, *85.*

Jews had attained as leaders in commerce.[1] As such, they had become indispensable to the people. Upon occasion even the stringency of the Feudal law was relaxed in their favor, that they might freely engage in the country's commerce. The general statement of Roscher[2] is applicable also here: "Es haben die Juden im frühen Mittelalter ein grosses Bedürfniss der Volkswirtschaft befriedigt, welches lange Zeit kein Anderer befriedigen konnte; das Bedürfniss eines gewerbmässigen Handelstriebes." They were the commercial intermediaries acceptable to both Christian and Moslem, to the one who demanded the products of the Orient and to the other who controlled the lands that produced the luxuries,—since they had no religious affiliation with either.[3] Even in more barbarous sections of the mediaeval world, it was not unusual to find the non-enforcement of restrictive measures against them, and for the same reason. "Il faut croire" says Bédarride,[4] "qu'il était plus facile aux rois visigothes, avec la haine le plus féroce contre les Juifs, de concevoir de pareilles lois que de les faire exécuter. Il manquait à ces mésures, la sanction donnée par les populations au milieu desquelles les Juifs étaient répandus. Or ces populations avaient besoin des services que leur rendirent les Juifs par leur industrie." The same explanation is to be given, according to Depping,[5] for the marked favor shown by Louis le Débonnaire to the Jews, and for the refusal of the authorities of Lyons to enter into the persecution demanded by Agobard,[6] insisting upon a rigorous separation of Jews from Christians. "Comment aurait on opéré

---

[1] Jacobs, *Jewish Contributions to Civilization, 190.*

[2] Roscher, *Ansichten der Volkswirtschaft, II 327.*

[3] Cunningham, *Western Civilization, II 49.*

[4] Bédarride, *32.*

[5] *Les Juifs dans le Moyen Age, 45.*

[6] Agobard, *De Insolentia Judaeorum, 61.* "Die Juden im Westreiche hatten mächtige Beschützer bei Hofe- schon gegen Agobard, und so geschah es dass zu Epernay auch der wider sie gerichtete Artikel des Konzils keine Aufnahme fand." Dümmler, *Gesch. des Ostfränkischen Reichs, I. 281.*

Kaiser Ludwig, 828, giebt einigen Kaufleuten ein Privilegium; er bestimmt —dass niemand sie beunruhigen oder verleumden—soll; 'sed liceat eis sicut Judaeis, partibus palatii nostri fideliter deservire.'

Aronius, *Regesten zur Gesch. der Juden im fränkischen und deutschen Reiche bis zum Jahre 1273 (1902).*

cette séparation au neuvième siècle dans une ville commerçante que Lyon, sans rompre les liens les plus doux de la société?" And later when their supremacy was challenged in the middle of the tenth century by the growth of the commercial spirit in the republic of Venice,[1] and its government enacted a law forbidding the masters of ships to give passage to Jewish merchants and others (strangers), as a measure of protection against powerful competitors, the law long remained a dead letter.[2]

Before the spirit of competition asserted itself, they must have been unhampered in their trade enterprises, both as agents and as artisans. Their commercial activity was especially noticeable in the silk industry, which because of the luxurious demands of Byzantium for its wares, was preeminent. An authority[3] on the social and economic conditions of the Empire aptly says, "zweifellos war die Seidenindustrie in Constantinopel eine der wichtigsten wenn nicht die wichtigste überhaupt. Der Bedarf an Seidenstoffen war ein ganz ungeheurer für den Kaiser, seine Familie, seinen Hof, die Kirche u. s. w., die bei der orientalischen Hofhaltung ebenfals in reicher Menge verwendet wurden. Heyd (Lev. Handel I 22) bemerkt mit Recht, 'Je weniger man durch Machtentfaltung imponiren konnte, desto mehr bedurfte man solcher Mittel (Prachtentfaltung) um die Ueberlegenheit des Römerreichs ausser Zweifel zu setzen.'" From Greece, where the Jews of mediaeval Europe had achieved their first and notable success as planters of mulberry trees, breeders of silk-worms, weavers and dyers of silk and purple fabrics, they carried the art into Sicily, and became its chief promoters and artisans there. Roger of Naples engaged Jewish experts from Greece to develop the industry in his kingdom. From Sicily it was easily transmitted to Italy where it was developed with equal skill and enterprise.[4] As a result the popular mind so closely identified

[1] Jacobs, *Jewish. Contr. to Civilization, 200.*

[2] Bédarride, *106 ff.*

[3] Stöckle, *Spätrömische u. byzant. Zünfte, 32.*

[4] Krauss, *Studien 73,* "Die Einführung der Seiden Zucht im griechisch-römischen Osten war eine Tat von welthistorischer Bedeutung, die dem Kaiser Justinianos zu verdanken ist, und nichts zeugt so sehr von der Vitalität der Juden als die Tatsache dass sie die ersten waren die sich in der neuen Kunst

the Jews with this industry that "the Jewish tax in Southern
Europe was sometimes called 'Tignta Judaeorum' as it was
levied as an impost on dyed goods."[1] By virtue of their
success in this local manufacture and traffic they would naturally
be in control of the commerce in such products from the richer
sources in the Orient. Men so well bearing the responsibilities
of a generally acknowledged source of renown and wealth, would,
from the mere sense of material gain, be favored as a valuable
asset of emperor and people. Such favor we should expect to
find as the portion of the communities in the great cities of Apulia,
whose surpassing commercial and maritime advantages domi-
nated the social order.

As far, then as the Jewish communities in the populous
mediaeval coast-towns of southern Italy are concerned, and
that of Constantinople as well, the chief commercial port of the
middle ages, it may justly be said that "geography[2] makes the
history of Lower Italy in the early mediaeval centuries"; the
interests developed by it are paramount. Ahimaaz' coherent
story of prosperity telling of these very communities is laid in
a world that is free in its familiarity with the masters and the
traffic of the sea. The outburst of fanaticism with which it
begins he finds difficult to understand. But its raging is only
that of a passing storm. For the moment, ecclesiastical interests
prevail. With the exception of its accounting for this persecution as the cruel policy of Basil and for the succeeding toleration
as the noble practice of Leo, both resulting from an imperial
edict, the chronicle gives the impression that the oppression
of Basil was followed by the clemency of Leo, not only for the
years of his reign, but for the entire period of this family's
experience.

Ascribing to Leo an edict that restored religious liberty may
well have been the simplest way of explaining to themselves what
the chronicler's ancestors must have seen. They may have
believed that only by such positive administrative measure could

so sehr auszeichneten." Pertz, *Mon. V 192;* Graetz, *5, 256;* R. Straus, *Die
Rechtsverhältnisse der Juden in Königreich Sizilien im 12 u. 13 Jahrhundert.*

[1] Abrahams, *Jewish Life in M. A., 219.*

[2] Curtis, *Roger of Sicily and the Normans in Lower Italy, 3.*

the change in their condition have been made. They attribute
to him a policy that is not only not expressly stated, but not
even implied in the severe measures pertaining to the Jews in the
additions to the Byzantine Code, which, by the consensus of
opinion among scholars, are ascribed to him. Realities of life
‚s the Jewish subjects of that Emperor were living it, may have
determined their interpretation, regardless of the text of the
Code which was probably inaccessible to them. By this attitude
towards Leo, the tradition gives impetus to the discussion that
hinges upon the disparity between the legislation of the Empire
and the social order that arises in defiance of it, a discussion that
arises generally in the consideration of the position of the Jews
in mediaeval society, but particularly in the study of the Byzantine phase of the question. The legislation of the codes is quite
frequently an unreliable index to the life which it is supposed to
control. Restricting himself to the evidence of Byzantine laws
concerning the Jews, Graetz[1] concludes that Byzantium was the
source from which all thought and practice of European persecution of the Jews emanated. Disputing this generalization,
Roscher,[2] arguing more safely and comprehensively from actual
communal life in the empire, observes, "War doch in Byzanz die
Überlieferung aus dem Alterthume niemals völlig unterbrochen
gewesen, und diese Staat Während des ganzen frühern Mittel-
alters der erste Handelsplatz der Christenheit!"

The imperial restrictions are not generally enforced to the
letter. It is as true of this Basilian period as it is of the preceding
centuries of Byzantine administration that the codes tell only
a part of the social story, at times a negligible part, having little
more than antiquarian value as religious and political proscrip-
tions decreed by an imperial will seeking to impose itself upon
the life of the people, but eventually, through indifference or
popular compulsion or material self-interest, permitting them
to be honored rather in the breach than in the observance.
There can be no question that "if the legal status of the Jews
were our sole criterion, the picture of their relations with medi-

[1] *Geschichte 8, 204.*
[2] *Ansichten der Volkswirtschaft, II, 335.*

aeval Christians would need to be painted in very sombre hues."[1]
A spirit of excessive ecclesiastical zeal now and then dictated
laws that could not be enforced because of powerful social forces
that opposed them. The problem resolves itself into a determination of the result of a contest between rigid legalism and
practical life. There is a wide diversity in the application of the
code, even when it is transmitted without change from one reign
to another.

An important contributing cause was, as Reinach points out,
the disposition of the various emperors.[2] Constance, a very
zealous patron of orthodoxy, in his use of the Constitutions of his
father, Constantine, wields an instrument of fanatic antagonism
which was altogether wanting when these civil and political
regulations were first applied. Theodosius II., less given to
ecclesiasticism, though adding to the civil disabilities of the
Jews, does not deprive them of religious freedom. A century
later, Justinian, with a passion for imperial regulation and in
his submission to the church, adds to the code the first religious
proscription, violating the liberty of Judaism, as a "religio
licita." Leo the Isaurian, aiming to conciliate the orthodox
accusers that charge him with heresy, and with being the
creature of the Jews in the shattering of the images, decrees
that all Jews and the remaining Montanists in Asia Minor must
submit to baptism (723). Similarly Basil I., his hands stained
with the crime through which he obtained the throne, readily
yields to the will of his ecclesiastical counsellors, and finds
nothing more acceptable to God than the extermination of all
heresy and, first of all, that form of it represented by Judaism.
But by the side of these representatives of political and religious
violence, the administrators who ruled in a spirit of clemency
and even of deliberate humanity are the more numerous among
Byzantine sovereigns.[3] Under Jovian, Valens and Valentinian,
Julian, Irene and Leo VI., the proscriptive measures were either
indifferently enforced or altogether disregarded. Theoretically,[4]

---

[1] Abrahams, J. Life in M. A., 399.

[2] Histoire, 43.

[3] Reinach, Diaspora JE, IV, 572; —Histoire, 43; Graetz, 5, 18.

[4] Berliner, II, 6, "Wie unter Theoderich genossen die Juden unter der

textually, the law of the land is essentially the same from the constitutions of Constantine to the Basilica, the last of the imperial codes.

One readily observes the terseness and the clearness with which the chronicle alludes to the character of Basil.[1] He was a man of treachery, a murderer; he was a worshipper of images; in other words, he began by showing traits of a bigoted mind, capable of a policy of persecution. It sees a direct connection between his superstitious orthodoxy and the ruthless conversionist scheme that he thrust upon the state. It is the one instance of such affliction recalled by his ancestors or by Ahimaaz, out of their own experience, in the course of the two hundred years of Basilian rule. It is thought of rather as a wild departure from the law of the empire than as a natural adherence to it. And the emperor who has commanded it, can nullify the edict at will, to spare entire communities.[2] There is actually but one instance in Byzantine History that might have served as a precedent for Basil's persecution: the violent heresy-hunting of Leo the Isaurian, through which Jewish communities in Constantinople[3] and other cities may have temporarily ceased to exist. He may have followed his example as he adopted the legislation of that emperor's Ecloga. Finlay's[4] criticism of its proscriptive measures, that they are rather a series of edicts than laws, may well be applied to the stringent regulations in the Basilica. It can scarcely be questioned that the later lawgiver, with all his denunciation of his predecessor as an arch heretic pulling down the sacred images, "servilely imitated all his political plans." Every reaction against and recovery from political and social chaos was signalized by a codification of the laws on the part of the emperor that was responsible for the restoration of imperial power. It may have been prompted both by a sense of need and, as far as later emperors are concerned, by

ganzen Herrschaft der Ostgothen bei Aufrechterhaltung der Gesetze des Theodosianischen Gesetzbuches eine vollständige Toleranz." Finlay, *II, 60, 148.*

[1] Below, *69.*

[2] Below, *73.*

[3] Broydé, *Constantinople, JE, IV, 237.*

[4] Finlay, *II. 33;* Zachariae, *Historiae Juris Graeco-Rom. Delineatio 14ff.*

an ambition to be ranked with the lawgivers. It is always practically the same code. The code begun by Basil and completed
by Leo and Constantine VII. is no exception to the rule. "Les
Basiliques contiennent, presque mot pour mot les articles du
code de Justinien. La jurisprudence est donc fixée à l'égard
des Juifs dès le sixième siècle. S'il êut diversité dans la politique
des Empereurs à leur égard, ce fut plutôt dans l'application des
lois existantes que dans la promulgation de nouveaux décrets."[1]

As far as Basil's codification is concerned, we are not left to
conjecture as to what the need and aim were, at least as understood by the author of the Life of Basil. Upon such authority,
Mortreuil[2] believes that upon Basil's accession to the throne,
there was "un cri général en faveur de la reforme des lois civiles
de toute parte dans l'empire; heureusement l'empereur, après
avoir par ses victoires relevé ses sujets de l'abattement profond
où ils étaient plongés depuis tant d'années, fut lui-même au-
devant des besoins qu' exigeaient l'administration de la justice,
et s'occupa de suite du sort déplorable de la legislation. Le
biographe inconnu qui a écrit sous Constantine Porphyrogénète
la vie de notre empereur s'exprime en ces termes: 'Trouvant les
lois civiles obscures et embrouillées à cause de mélange des
bons et des mauvaises dispositions, car les lois abrogées comme
celles en vigueur figuraient sans distinction dans un seul et même
corps de droit, Basile régularisa leur condition avec autant
de soin que l'entreprise le comportait. À cet effet, il élimina
les lois abrogées qui se trouvaient sans application, il revisa le
grand nombre de celles qui avaient un intérêt d'actualité, et
pour faciliter l'étude de ces dernières, il réduisit, leur nombre
infini dans un abrégé divisé en chapitres particuliers." And
Basil gives his own view of his legislative work, in the preface
of his first digest of the laws:[3] "As for the ancient laws, we have
gathered, in a single volume, all those that have been abrogated,
so that they may be known of all, and that there invalidity may
be manifest. The laws that are still valid, we have arranged
in another compilation."

[1] Janin, *Echos d'Orient*, (1912).
[2] Mortreuil, *Histoire du Droit byzantin*, *II*, *19*.
[3] Brandileone, *Prochiron*.

5

Whatever the intention, as expressed in these words, may have been, the labor of revision did not produce a code, in any important respect, different from the established work of Justinian. The laws concerning Jews,[1] as a whole, are those of the older code. They contain the same provisions to shield the Christians against the Jews, originally devised, probably, to oppose menacing Jewish proselytism, and the regulations to protect the Jews against the fanatic zeal of Christians. Basil's violent conversionist policy is in flagrant contradiction to the law incorporated in the Basilica,[2] "No Jew shall be persecuted because he is a Jew; his religion shall not be a pretext for harassing him." (Bas. L, 144; Code l. g. 14); "All damage done to the property of Jews shall be compensated by double payment; the governors of the cities and provinces who permit such offenses, are liable to the same penalty. Under penalty of excommunication, no one shall desecrate the synagogs by military billeting." The law also ordains respect for the Sabbath and the Jewish Feasts; On these days no Jew shall be asked to labor or serve in any curial capacity. Clearly, the years of relentless oppression described by Ahimaaz bear no relation to these quite equitable requirements of the imperial code. Janin's comment on these protective measures, transmitted from the earliest constitutions of the Empire, is eminently applicable to this period of persecution; "Sérieusement appliqués, ces édits de protection auraient rendu la situation d'Israel en somme fort tolérable." This imperial mission to the Jews is in utter violation of them all. It is dictated not by the desire, originally responsible for them, to restrain and humiliate the Jews through civil and political disabilities, but by a determination to destroy their religion, root and branch; a mission passionately conceived as the first of the three great tasks that Basil imposed upon himself.

The Jewish chronicler leaves no doubt as to the bitterness and the extent[3] of the calamity that resulted, that became

---

[1] Reinach, *Diaspora JE;* Cassel, *Ersch und Gruber, Die Juden, 52;* Scherer, *Die Rechtsverhältnisse d. Juden, I, 3.*

[2] *Echos d'Orient, 1912.*

[3] Below, *73.*

the frequent subject of penitential poems and, among the mediaeval Jews, became the sorrowful memory of the "five communities that were spared and of the thousand that were martyred."
In this Jewish tradition it is raging intolerance on the part of
the dominant religion against a persistent rival. The votary
of Judaism must become a member of the church, confessing that
"Jesus is the fulfilment of the Law and the Prophets," [1] as the
Byzantine authors express the controlling thought of Basil.
The Byzantine histories[2] of this event likewise accentuate the
sectarian prompting that was responsible for it. Among modern
students of the reign of Basil, there is a tendency to insist too
strongly upon the distinction between political, economic and
religious interests as we have come to know them, and to
attribute his repression of the Jews to other than ecclesiastical
motives. Under the conspicuous leadership of the Emperor,
the avowed patron of orthodoxy, aspiring to remove every trace
of the Iconoclast heresy, the lurking hostility to Judaism would
have every encouragement to throw off restraint; there would
naturally be but one criterion of loyalty to the state—adherence
to the orthodox creed. That his edict was so intended and was
so understood, is evident from the biographies and chronicles,
that, for this excessive missionary zeal, proclaim him the acceptable representative of imperial power.

Whatever consideration might have been given to various
spheres of administration in his day, the testimony of this Jewish
document, and that of the Christian sources are at one in proving

[1] Krauss, *Studien* 42.

[2] "Videns autem nulla re sic Deum delectari ut animorum salute, eumque
qui dignum ab indigno educat Christi os nuncupari (Jer. 15, 19) neque apos-
tolicum opus hoc sibi negligendum segniusve habendum putavit. Sed ante
omnia Judaeorum gentem incircumcisum et duro corde ac cervice quod in
ipso fuit, in Christo obsequium verbi sagena, irretiit. Jubens enim suae
religionis argumentis allatis disputationibus aleam experiri acvel sua firma
ostendere et quibus contradici non possit aut persuasos Christum legis caput
esse et prophetarum." Theophanes Contin. 345.

"Imperii annis septimo et octavo baptizat Basilius Hebraeos omnes sub
dicione positas, dignitatibus augens ac plura illis dona tribuens."

Symeonis Magistri, *Annales*, 691; Georgii Monachi, *Vitae Imperatorum
Recentiorum*, 9.

that the ecclesiastical interests were paramount during this reign, with civic and economic considerations severely subordinated to them, if not entirely ignored. For the time being, the more tolerant spirit of social cooperation that generally manifested itself in Byzantine life to the discomfiture of lawless ecclesiasticism, had gone down to defeat. Unlike those sovereigns who had similar conversionist designs but were thwarted by the unwilling populace, or by generally untoward conditions, from carrying them out, the founder of the Macedonian dynasty attained success that continued as long as he reigned. It is therefore going very far afield to see in this anti-Jewish policy not a proscription of Judaism but a repression of the Jews for economic and political reasons. In a comprehensive and scholarly study of the reign of Basil, Vogt[1] calls attention to the wide diffusion of heresies in the empire, to the communities of Jews, Samaritans, Paulicians,[2] and to Monophysites and other Christian Sectaries that disputed the authority of the Greek church; he is of the opinion that the Jews, rather than the more menacing, yet more remote, Paulicians, were the first body attacked, because they were within easier reach in their large settlements in Constantinople and other cities under his immediate jurisdiction. He finds, so far as legislation is concerned, a relaxation of tyranny in their favor: "Le fait le plus curieux concernant les Juifs au neuvième siècle est assurément la relative douceur de la législation à leur égard. Basile ne parle pas des peines qu'attendent les Juifs apostats. Il ne parait pas avoir édicté à leur usage des lois aussi sévères que pour les manichéens. Il se contente de prévenir leur zèle religieux en les empêchant de faire de la propagande. D'Après le Prochiron, le Juif n'était puni de mort qu'en deux circonstances, s'il imposait la circoncision à son esclave chrétien, et s'il cherchait à le détourner de la foi orthodoxe." [3] He plainly assumes that there was a strict adherence to the letter of the law.

But the political factor which he emphasizes is proven a negligible one from his own words, when he traces the causes of

---

[1] Vogt, *Bas. 1, 295.*

[2] Finlay, *II, 169, 243ff;* Vogt, *ibid., 322.*

[3] Vogt, *ibid., 304.*

this bitter antagonism to the Jews, to earlier conditions of toleration, especially under Michael of Amorion,[1] when they ventured upon widespread proselytism[2] in the Empire, arousing the clergy to redouble their opposition, to seize just such an opportunity as Basil's patronage offered. In addition to traditional and historical antipathies, which he finds insufficient to explain the violent policy, he accepts another reason which Photius had given in a letter to Michael of Bulgaria: "They allied themselves with all other heretics,"[3] as is implied also in the closing words of the formula for the reception of a Jew into Christianity, "Anathème non seulement à la doctrine israélite mais encore à toutes les doctrines hérétiques." In these details of his study, Vogt lays bare the weakness of the political theory as to the position of the Jews under Basil. After all, he who lays so much stress upon the text of the laws accepts the fact that is not sanctioned by them, and that is known only through the writings of those who, either as contemporaries or as later compilers of tradition, vouched for it; and his attitude in the end, is actually that which one would reasonably adopt when confronted with such conflicting documentary evidence. To offset the testimony of the code, we have the doubly effective evidence, on the one hand, of Theophanes Continuatus and the other historians representative of the orthodoxy of the age; on the other, of the record of affliction transmitted by the descendants of those who were brought to the verge of annihilation. These together give the data of prime importance in forming our judgment of the situation. Taking them at their historical value, we may well conclude, with Krauss,[4] that "Basil affected the Jews as no other Greek Emperor had done." In the light of the family annals of Ahimaaz, Basil, in his intolerance, is a solitary figure among the sovereigns of the Macedonian dynasty.

[1] Finlay II, *128*.

[2] "Fuit hic Michaelus Amorii natus, superioris Phrygiae urbe; in qua ab antiquis temporibus Judaeorum Athinganorum aliorumque impiorum multitudo habebat . . . erat Michaelo praeceptor . . . Ebraeus quidam (sive is femina potius Ebraica fuit)." Cedrenus (Bekker), *69, 4*.

[2] Rambaud, *Études*, *272*.

[3] Vogt, *Bas. 1*, *302*. Migne, *PG I 1465;* Cumont, *Wiener Studien, 1902, 24*.

[4] Krauss, *Byz. Empire JE III 453*.

Of specific importance as a supplementary and corroborative
document for the history of Basil's reign, this collection of
Jewish traditions serves as a unique contribution to our knowledge of that of Leo VI. It stands alone in accrediting this
emperor with a radical departure from his predecessor's policy
of persecution.[1] Its emphatic, positive statement leaves nothing
to speculation; there is in it no such omission as that of the
official histories that mention the return of many apostates to
their Jewish faith, after the death of Basil,[2] adding no word of
explanation of so strange a fact; leaving to conjecture, whether
it was caused by the annulment of the edict of persecution.
Instead of being counted among the Byzantine emperors who
made "lettre morte" of the more humane provisions of religious
toleration, he is to be ranked, by the insistence of these beneficiaries, among the princes of toleration. We must accept
it as a trustworthy statement, so far, at least, as the outstanding
experience of religious freedom is concerned. It is so regarded
by Broydé when he says: "No wonder that Constantinople
became the centre of Judaism when Leo VI. restored religious
freedom to the Jews."[3] The happier conditions may well have
warranted the belief that the cruel edict had been formally
and officially annulled.

The adoption of this tradition does indeed involve us in difficulties if we insist that the stringent measures in the Basilica,
attributed to Leo, must remain the chief, if not the only source
of information as to the character of his administration. If, for
instance, we accept as the controlling authority in the study
of his reign, the inaugural declaration reported of him, that, to
prove worthy of his royal inheritance, he would not only continue
the departed emperor's attack upon heresy, but would even add
to its violence; if we accept it as conclusive in the valuation of
testimony bearing upon his life, we shall have insuperable diffi-

[1] Below, 74.

[2] Return of the Jews to their faith upon the death of Basil I is mentioned
by Theophanes Continuatus, 341, "Multos . . . ad Christi fidem attraxit,
quanquam plerique rursum post imperatorem e vivis exemptum, ad vomitem
suum ut canes reversi sunt."

[3] Broydé, *Constantinople, JE. IV, 237*.

culty with the statement of Ahimaaz that flatly contradicts it. Krauss,[1] attempting to reconcile the evidence of the code and that of the Jewish tradition, suggests that, among the violent measures of Leo, there may, at least, not have been the decree of compulsory baptism; or, that there may have been a brief respite between the declaration of the close of Basil's reign and the enthronement of his successor, during which interval of suspended administration the victims of persecution might have thrown off the mask of orthodoxy, which, however, they might again have been compelled to wear when he was seated in authority.

We may obtain a more satisfactory result if we restrict each of these authorities to its own sphere, in the one instance, to the theory of official legislation, in the other, to the facts of social experience. In other words, we must choose between the literal proof of the laws and the photographic record of life. Whereas, under Basil's rule, the severity becomes the arbitrary practice promulgated by a zealot nature, the praise for toleration might have been bestowed upon Leo, for laxity in the enforcement of repressive measures; a laxity that may even have been forced upon him. There is no reason to believe that the continuity of administration was broken as he succeeded to the throne. Basil, filled with the ambition of establishing a dynasty, and following Byzantine custom, had guarded against such contingency, by crowning[2] his sons in their childhood, proclaiming their incontestable right to the throne. Leo was thus chosen for imperial power in his infancy. Upon the death of Constantine, the eldest son of Basil, Leo naturally became heir apparent. "Vita functo Constantino, tum amor et spes omnis in Leonem." [3] Again, the inscription of the first digest of laws of the new era inaugurated by Basil, the Prochiron, in which the joint authorship and sovereignty of the father and two sons are clearly proclaimed, gives further assurance of the improbability of any interregnum.

[1] Krauss, *Studien*, 44 n. 8.
[2] Finlay, *II*, 256.
  Zonaras, *II 167*, "Filios tres Constantinum, Leonem et Alexandrum augustalibus coronis ornavit."
  McCabe, *Empresses of Cple*, 123.
[3] Lupus Protospatarius.

And with equal clearness the annals of Lupus Protospatarius imply the continuity of imperial rule, specifying that the sons' reign of twenty-six years in their own right followed immediately upon that of nine years which they had shared with their father. Furthermore, a fleeting interlude of privileged existence would not account for the sense of unbounded relief and gratitude that the words of the Chronicle convey.

While it is generally believed that Leo not only succeeded to his father's throne, but also carried to completion his legislative plans; that he had been disciplined and pledged to do so; such an estimate falls far short of covering his entire career. The younger basileus could not have been merely another Basil, of somewhat smaller and feebler stature. He has individuality; to the people of his time he was the Sage, the Philosopher, the only Byzantine emperor so designated. We should hesitate to question the sincerity of the tribute, and doubt the merit, as it was understood in his day, that elicited such praise. It seems an extreme generalization to dispose of it as the meaningless verbiage of flattering courtiers and truckling chroniclers;[1] to say as does Kremer,[2] that "Leo had no right to the title either through his public or his private life." Whatever the reason for this exceptional designation, whether he owes it to his prolific theological writings[3] or to general authorship, or to pronounced interest in the study of philosophy and liberal patronage of its teachers, there probably was some conspicuous trait that suggested the surname. At any rate, there is in it the suggestion of less aggressive qualities than those of the ambitious reorganizer of declining Byzantine power.[4] He may well have been a worthy pupil, as Mortreuil believes, of Photius the teacher of his youth: "Les leçons de cet homme ne furent pas sans influence sur l'esprit du disciple. Laborieux, actif, Léon aima passionnément l'étude et travailla avec persévérance au bonheur de ses

[1] Graetz, 5, 245.

[2] Kremer, Culturgeschichte d. Orients unter d. Chalifen, II, 23.

[3] Krumbacher, Gesch. d. byz. Lit., 628, 721; Sandys, I, 396; Finlay, II, 259.

[4] Gelzer, Das Verhältniss von Staat und Kirche in Byzanz, Historische Zeits N. F. 50, 193.

sujets. Malheureusement ses moeurs dissolues imprimèrent une tache odieuse sur sa conduite privée. Il ne fut pas heureux dans ses expeditions militaires. Les Sarrasins lui enlevèrent Samos et Thessalonique. Les Bulgares ravagèrent la Thrace sous les yeux. Sentant alors la faiblesse des forces effectives de l'empire, il se replia sur la diplomatie et il parvint, en mettant en jeu les ressorts de la politique, à passer en paix le reste de son regne."

Graetz,[1] upon the evidence of the Novellae, having charged Leo with more savage intolerance than that of Basil, wavers in his opinion, when he becomes aware of the large settlements of Jews in the Byzantine Empire upon the death of Leo. A relentless Byzantine Inquisition would have shattered the foundations needed for such thriving life. Finlay sees a radical difference between the administration of Leo and that of Basil, when he holds him responsible for undermining the entire system of Basilian legislation.[2] The appearance of such a work as the "Book of the Prefect"[3] among the important writings of Leo testifies to a strong sense of social and economic organization. Its survey of the world of trade and commerce in the Empire betrays no sign of the existence of a spirit of rampant ecclesiasticism. Whether, then, the violent hand of Basilian Government was restrained by turbulence through the attacks of powerful invaders, or by the predominance of economic interests over the ecclesiastical, or by the deliberate interposition of the emperor, decreeing the end of persecution, the tradition of the forefathers of Ahimaaz, that under Leo, of blessed memory to them, their religious freedom was restored, carries conviction. And to the end of the record, whether it tells of their life in the Empire or in the provinces of the Caliphate, that privilege is not again denied them.

At the conclusion of this study we are constrained to approve

[1] Graetz, *5, 245*. Novella 55 upon which the general statement is based, in the Latin version of Krüger, *Corpus Juris III 798*, reads, "Nos igitur quod pater noster praetermisit, id complendum esse recte putantes, omni antiquiori quae de Hebraeis statuit legi silentium iniungimus, et ne illi aliter, quam pura et salutaris christianorum fides vult, vivere audeant, jubemus.

[2] Finlay, II, *236, 261*.

[3] Nicole, *Le Livre de Prefet;* Stöckle, *Spätröm. u. byz. Zünfte.*

the protest of Krauss[1] against indifference to the Byzantine period of Jewish History and Literature. In this attitude Jewish scholars have no doubt followed the conspicuous leading of their Christian colleagues. Modern Byzantine studies[2] having begun quite auspiciously in the seventeenth century at the hands of Du Cange, under the patronage of Louis XIV., were almost completely abandoned in the following century, largely through the influence of Gibbon,[3] Lebeau and Montesquieu, to whom Byzantine history was but a dismal chapter of utter barbarism. So they languished until the latter half of the nineteenth century,[4] when amid exhaustive research in the history of the Middle Ages, interest in them was revived. From a new sense of their legitimate value, the world of scholarship has found them eminently worthy of attention. Through the labors of Diehl, Rambaud, Zacharie, Krumbacher, Finlay, Schlumberger and a host of others, Byzantine life is no longer an outlawed province of investigation. In the introduction to the second edition of Krumbacher's history of Byzantine Literature, published ten years after the first, he points to the larger volume, almost double the size of the earlier one, as telling evidence of the strides of the progress in the accumulation of material and in the pursuit of ·Byzantine studies. Apart from the stimulation that such fruitful labors give to the study of this period from the Jewish viewpoint, there is further incentive in the remains of that Mediaeval Jewish life that have been discovered in our day. They have independent value, as Kaufmann[5] remarks, speaking of the importance of the Geniza[6] documents; "Ganz besonders dankbar

---

[1] Krauss, *Studien*, "Unbekannt und unbeachtet steht diese Geschichte da und doch wird es sich zeigen dass sie in der Gesammtgeschichte der Judenheit sogar einen weiten Raum beanspruchen kann, nach dem Worte Kaufmann's, des feinfühligen Historikers, ist das byzantinische Reich der dunkle Erdteil der jüdischen Geschichte im Mittelalter."

[2] Diehl, *Les Études Byzantines en France, Byz. Zeits.* 1900. *Les Études d'Histoire Byzantine en 1901, Rev. de Synthèse Historique,* 1901.

[3] Voltaire, *Le Pyrrhonisme de l'Histoire, Ch. XV n. 1;* Lebeau, *Le Bas-Empire, Introd.;* Gibbon, *Ch. 48;* Montesquieu, *Considérations sur les Causes de la Grandeur des Romains, etc. 3 Ed. 1911, 195ff.*

[4] Diehl, in Rambaud's *Études.*

[5] Kaufmann, *Byz. Zeits,* 1898; Perles, *Byx. Z. 1893, 569.*

[6] Above, *32.*

muss hier jeder Trümmer begrüsst werden, der uns über Vorgänge in dem einst so weitgezogenen byzantinischen Reiche Nachrichten giebt die wir·in dem sonst so reichen griechischen Schrifttume vergeblich suchen würden."

The discovery of these collections of tradition, following so closely upon the publication of the Chronicle of Ahimaaz, that had already renewed the hope of penetrating the obscurity of Byzantine Jewish life, vindicated the theory of the pioneers in the study, that behind the veil there is a world of thriving life. Yet this promising field has comparatively few toilers to cultivate it. Krauss[1] pleads for greater interest in it, since it surely does not deserve to be a "friendless waif" among the interests of scholars. These manuscripts have already revealed enough to lead to the conclusion,[2] "Nous sommes maintenant fondés à rompre le silence méprisant que guardait Graetz à l'égard de ces rabbins italiens, à son sens médiocres ou non existants. Quand il écrivait, on savait bien peu de chose sur l'histoire des Juifs en Italie." For the clearest tradition thus far revealed, on the communal life over which these sages of Italy presided, we must turn to the chronicle of Ahimaaz.

[1] Krauss, *Studien 122*, "Die Literatur der Juden in griechischer Sprache ist überhaupt eine der schwierigsten Partieen der Literatur (Steinschneider *JQR 16, 383*). Gilt das von der alten hellenischen jüdischen Literatur, so mit noch mehr Recht von der byzantinisch-jüdischen Literatur; das Meisste liegt noch in Mss."

[2] Adler, *REJ 67, 40*.

PART II

A Book of Genealogies

In the name of the Lord, we will begin and finish (our task).   1*a
My help (cometh) from the Lord.

In the name of the Lord of Lords that doeth wonders I will
write a book of genealogies.

In the name of Him that dwelleth in the heavens of splendor,
I will begin to tell the story, diligently to investigate, arrange
and present a collection[1] of the traditions of my forefathers, to
unfold them in proper order, to explain them with notes, to trace
without confusion the genealogy whose parts must be collected
like stubble.   At the outset I will give praise and ascribe greatness to Him that is mighty in deeds.   I will glorify His holy
name, and ever extol His memorial; with awe and trembling I
will exalt Him, as from the days of old; I will be awake to declare
His glory and will not slumber, as with the words of my mouth,
I acknowledge the Eternal God is a dwelling place.   I seek favor
before the habitation of the Eternal God.   I pray in word and
thought that my supplication, fervent and sincere, may rise to
Him that dwelleth in heaven, that I may inculcate lessons of
truth, chant the prayers, and rise in song to the Lord of Lords,
in the seat of the elders, in the company of the learned; that, with
might, I may adore the Ever-living One, and in veneration,
magnify the Most High; that I may crown[2] with sovereignty Him
that dwelleth on high, in the assembly of the upright and the
meeting of the wise.   Day and night I will delight in praise to
Him that doeth great things, that soundeth with the thunder;
the Lord of Hosts, that worketh wonders, that did marvelous

* The marginal numbers and letters indicate the corresponding pages and
sections of the Hebrew text.

[1] Bacher, *REJ 32, 144ff.*; Abrahams, *Chapters on Jewish Literature, 79.*

[2] Talmud, *Aboda Zara 44a*; Kohut, *Aruch III 405b*; Kaufmann, *MGWJ
40, 29 n. 3.*

things for the guidance of my ancestors, that doeth marvelous things before my eyes, to instruct me, as signs and wonders, a promise of good. To Him that dwelleth in heaven, I will turn in joyful praise, to invoke Him in sacred melody, with the outpouring of entreaty, with reverence and understanding, with awe and becoming humility, like that of the lily of the valley; to proclaim His mighty deeds and to tell of His wonders, the power of His greatness, the splendor of His majesty, the endurance of His strength, the beauty of His eminence, the continuance of His wonders, the permanence of His dominion, which, to His praise, He hath marvelously created by His eternal power. He that established the mountains by His might, and that declareth unto man what is his thought; that created the earth by His wisdom and formed the world by His understanding, who in the heavens can be compared to Him whose kingdom extendeth to the ends of the earth? He causeth the sea to flee at His rebuke; the inhabitants of the world tremble for fear of Him; at His presence the mountains skip; under His gaze, the hills move. Truly great is His power, in all places is His dominion. Extolled and exalted be the splendor of His majesty; praised be His name and the name of His kingdom's glory.

With praise, I will glorify Him that dwelleth in heaven; that, in His grace and justice, safely guided my ancestors who came forth with the exiles[1] that were spared in Jerusalem, and delivered them from destruction, children and elders, young and old, for the sake of His great mercy and the merit of the fathers of old. At all times they were protected by the God of heaven; shield and buckler has He ever been to my forefathers, and so may He continue to be to their children to the last generation.

1b

Now, with great care, I will set down in order the traditions of my fathers, who were brought on a ship over the Pishon,[2] the first river of Eden, with the captives that Titus took from the Holy City, crowned with beauty. They came to Oria; they settled there and prospered through remarkable achievements; they grew in number and in strength and continued to thrive. Among

---

[1] Above, *10*.

[2] The reference may be to the Euphrates that the exiles crossed on their way to Italy. Neubauer assumes (*JQR IV, 614*) that the river in question is the Po.

their descendants there arose a man eminent in learning, a liturgical poet and scholar, master of the knowledge of God's law, distinguished for wisdom among his people. His name was Rabbi Amittai.[1] And he had a number of amiable and worthy sons, intelligent and learned men, scholars and poets zealously teaching, worthy disciples, men of merit and renown, masters of secret lore,[2] grasping and applying the deeper truth of scriptures; adepts in the mysteries, fathoming the veiled principles of Hokmah and Binah (Esoteric and Exoteric Wisdom) and of all abstruse learning; wise in the knowledge of the Book of Jashar,[3] and familiar with the hidden meaning of the Merkaba. The first of them was R. Shephatiah,[4] zealous in the pursuit of wisdom; the second, R. Hananeel,[5] engaged in the study of the Law of God which Jekutiel[6] (Moses) delivered; the third, Eleazar, who was devoted to (the Law) given in the third[7] (month). In the days of these good men there came from Bagdad, from our beloved ones, an esteemed man of distinguished family,[8] an illustrious scholar, warding off wrath from the descendants of those that

[1] Above, *11*.

[2] The clearly defined features of the mysticism of the author's day: the adroit cabalistical reading and application of Scripture; the contemplation of the mysteries of Hokmah and Binah, the masculine and feminine, or active and passive, principles of the fundamental Sefirot; wonder-working, and knowledge of the hidden truth of Divine Majesty (Merkaba). Bloch, *Die jüdische Mystik u. Kabbala, 255.*

[3] Preeminent among the cabalistical works of the later Geonic times. It is likewise placed at the head of the list of Hai Gaon (Ta-am Zekenim of Eliezer Ashkenasi, 56 b); Sefer Ha-Jashar, Harbah de Moshe, Raza Rabba, Sod Torah, Hekhalot Rabbati, Hekhalot Zutrati. Its authorship is attributed to R. Akiba by Zunz (*GV 179 n. a*).

[4] The ample traditions of this eldest son of Amittai establish his identity. Opposing the view of Zunz (*Literaturgeschichte, 4 note 7*), who at first regarded him as contemporary with the captives of Titus, and later (*Synagogale Poesie, 170; GV 405 note d*) believed him to be the author of a poem for Neila, flourishing in the time of the Byzantine Emperor Basil II. (976–1026), these records confirm the opinion of Graetz, that he lived in the reign of Basil I. (867–886).

[5] Zunz, *GV 375 note e, Lit. 345*; Kaufmann, *MGWJ 40, 507.*

[6] Kaufmann, *MGWJ 38, 237*; Neubauer, *MJC I, Sambari, 156.*

[7] Ginzberg, *The Legends of the Jews, III 77ff.*

[8] Neubauer, *JQR IV 615*; Zunz, *Ges. Schriften III 162*; Kaufmann, *MGWJ 40, 466 n. a.*; Talmud, *Sanhedrin 49a.*

sleep in Hebron; he was as of the (favored) flock[1] unto the Almighty King (King Adiriron).[2]

Before Aaron[3] left his native land, his father had a mill by which he supported himself. It was turned by a mule. A lion fell upon the mule and killed it, while Aaron was out of the room. When he returned he could not find the mule, so he put the lion in its place, and fastened him to the mill to turn the grinding stones. When his father saw what he had done, he approached him and exclaimed, "What hast thou done? Thou hast put in the lion: thou hast humiliated him and broken his strength. God made him king and intended him to walk erect, and thou hast forced him into thy service, to work for thee. Now, as God liveth, thou shalt not remain with me, thou shalt go into exile, wandering by day and by night, for three years thou shalt suffer punishment for this offense. At the end of that time return to thy native land, and the Lord thy God will accept thee."

2a

He came to Joppa. There he found ships on every hand. He said to the sailors, "Comrades and friends, in the name of God I come to you. I will go with you, and, with the favor of Him that dwelleth in light, will control fate, so that by the help of the awe-inspiring God, the ship on which we sail may not be over-taken by enemies or storm wind." He went in and took his place among them. At the hour for sleep they reached the city of Gaeta. There Aaron came upon a Jew, a Sephardi, who befriended him and proffered the hospitality of his home. At

2b

[1] Rosh haShana I, 2; Dembitz, *Services in Synagog and Home, 237*.

[2] One of the names of God evolved in the mysticism of the Piyyutim. Zunz, *SP 474.*

[3] This is the first of the Chronicle's graphic references to Aaron or Abu Aaron, which are now accepted as conclusive identification,—though the father's name is not given,—of Aaron ben Samuel ha-Nasi (Exilarch of Babylon 773–816), who, as a distinguished master of the learning of the schools of the Geonim, appeared and taught in the communities of Southern Italy about the middle of the ninth century. This authentic information disposes of the theory that he is a mythical figure invented to serve as the first master of prayer-interpretation and mysticism, believed by Eleazar of Worms and other commentators on the prayers to be the teacher of Moses ben Kalonymus who, among others, was called from Lucca to Mainz.

Graetz, *V 421;* Zunz, *SP 105;* Neubauer, *REJ 23, 23;* Eppenstein, *MGWJ 55, 733;* Neubauer, *MJC I, 41.*

meal time the Sephardi did not eat, though the day was the Sabbath, sacred unto God. The master, surprised at his conduct, said, "Today is the Sabbath unto the awe-inspiring One, why dost thou not delight thyself with that which is called a delight?" The unhappy man answered, "Oh my master, do not urge me, for I am very sad, I am grieving for my son who has been taken from me for my many sins; I do not really know whether he is alive or dead." The master then said to him in words of tenderness, "Observe the Sabbath properly, then show me the streets and lanes in which he used to come and go. If he be still alive, I will restore him to thee, and if dead, I will surely tell thee." The next day he did not delay. Together they went to the house of their friends that his son had frequently visited, and there they found a woman,[1] an accursed sorceress, practicing her sorcery. She had changed the boy into a mule and had bound him to the mill stones, to make him grind as long as he lived. When the sage saw him, he recognized him and understood, and said to the father, "See, thy son, whom thou hast thought dead, is restored to thee." He then spoke to the woman, and rebuking her, said, "Why art thou not overwhelmed with shame, since thou art caught in the net? Give back to the father his son, his own flesh." The wicked woman was crestfallen; she did not give heed to his words and did not answer him either gently or harshly. Thereupon the good man took hold of the mule, led him out, transformed him, gave him his original form, and restored him to his father. The master turned in praise to his Maker. Together they uttered praise to their God, their Creator.

After this (incident), he made use of his wonder-working   3a
wisdom, to do very difficult and astonishing things. When he reached Beneventum the entire community came out as one man to welcome him. On the Sabbath, an esteemed young man arose to read the prayers before Him that dwelleth on high. He chanted with pleasing voice. When he reached the words "Barechu et adonai hammevoroch," his voice lingered on the sound, but he did not pronounce God's name. The master at once realized that the reader was actually a dead man, and (it

[1] Blau, *Das Altjüdische Zauberwesen, 23;* Lenormant, *La Magie, 70.*

is known that) the dead do not praise God. "Stop," he at once commanded in a loud voice, "Do not give praise, for thou art not permitted to recite prayer before God." Then he began to question the youth, to plead with him in the name of his Maker, saying, "Tell me and do not fear, do not conceal from me what thou hast done, confess the truth before the Creator of the Spirit, glorify the God of glory, give thanks to Him in the midst of the congregation, and so acquire a portion in the world to come, and in this (world) be without sin. Thou wilt then be free from transgression, winning for thyself blessings, the well-ordered world (to come), and the good appointed for the righteous among His people, for those that fear God and honor His name." Immediately he answered, "I have indeed sinned, and trespassed against God; I have rebelled and transgressed and done wrong. If you are willing to bear the burden of the sin which your servant has committed, (I will confess). And all of them were willing to bear all that he imposed upon them. Thereupon he confessed, giving thanks to God; and thus told what he had done and what had happened to him. He said:

Hear me, oh people of God, my teachers and masters, leaders and elders, sages and scholars, princes and nobles, old and young, I will tell you plainly all that happened.

In my time[1] there was a Jew named R. Ahimaaz who went to Jerusalem, the glorious city, three times, to fulfil his vow. On each pilgrimage he took 100 pieces of gold [2] with him, as he had vowed to the Rock of his salvation, to give aid to those who were engaged in the study of His law, and to those who mourned the ruined house of His glory. As he set out on his third pilgrimage, he asked my mother for me, saying, "Let him go with me, to keep me company and help me on the way. I will bring him back to thee; at my hands thou mayest require him; if I do not bring him back to thee, I shall have sinned before God, I and my children." Then we set out on our journey rejoicing, without a thought of sadness. As we were sitting at the table of the scholars in study with the head of the academy, the teachers of the Law exclaimed, "Let us give praise, in pleasant and fervent song, with love and devotion to Him that is adored by myriads." They looked at their disciples seated before them; the head of their school turned to them and said, "Let the young man in our midst, who has come with our colleague R. Ahimaaz, cheer us and delight our heart with the flow of his knowledge and the utterance of his thoughts." Then I began reverently to give praise in psalm and song to Him that putteth on light as a garment.

3b

---

[1] Kaufmann, *468.*

[2] Schechter, *Studies in Judaism, I 350;* Krauss, *Studien, 109.*

There sat one of the elders in meditation, intently listening to my chanting.   3c
He began to weep bitterly. R. Ahimaaz, looking at him, noticed his actions,
and arising from the company went over to him and begged him to tell why
he wept. The elder simply told him that God had decreed that, in a little
while, the young man would surely die. When the good man heard this his
eyes filled with tears, he rent his clothes and tore out his hair, and exclaimed
before them all, "I have no place among the living; I have sworn to his mother
that I would bring him back to her, without mishap or harm; how can I
return to my house, if the lad is not with me? The oath which I have taken
will be the means of blighting my hope and ardent expectation." See-
ing his affliction and his bitter weeping, they wrote the Holy Name that
was written in the Sanctuary; they made an incision in the flesh of my right
arm, and inserted the Name[1] where the flesh had been cut. So I came away
in peace and returned home to my mother. While R. Ahimaaz was alive I
wandered[2] from land to land. Living since that time, I can live forever if
I so desire, for no man can know the place of the Name unless I reveal it.
But I will show it to you; I am in your hands; deal with me as seems right in
your eyes.

So they brought the grave clothes; he approached and put
them on; he then showed where the master had made the
incision, and took the Name out of it. His body became lifeless;
the corpse crumbled in decay as from the dissolution of many
years, the flesh returned to the dust.

From that city he (Aaron) journeyed onward and went to   4a
Oria.[3] There he found tents (of study), set up by the rivers,
planted and thriving like trees by the waters, schools established,

---

[1] Blau, *117*.

[2] Upon this passage Bacher bases the opinion that it contains the first
mention of the legend of the wandering Jew. But the story here told is
fundamentally different. In this instance, the wanderer has knowledge of the
miraculous power that keeps him alive, and is free to make an end of its
sway over him, by telling his dread secret as, in weariness and with a sense of
guilt, he finally does. Furthermore, the continuance of life is here bestowed
in a spirit of paternal sympathy and kindness, and not inflicted, as with
Ahasuerus or Bottadeus of the popular legend, as endless punishment for
a monstrous offense. L. Neubaur, *Die Sage vom ewigen Juden.*

[3] These traditions regarding Oria as a seat of learning in the ninth century,
affording especially favorable conditions for the activities of Abu Aaron, tell
more clearly what is suggested in the occasional references of Shabbethai
Donnolo to the city as his birthplace and a centre of Jewish life. The name
in the earlier source could not have referred (Zunz *GV 375*) to Aversa (founded
by the Normans in 1027). It is explained by Adler (*REJ 67, 40*) as a genitive
form. It is probably the transliteration of a word used by the Byzantine
writers. In the Chronicon Lupi Protospatarii (Migne *PL 155, 141*), the city
is mentioned as Ories Civitas, and again, indicating the genitive form, Civi-
tatem Oriae. Krauss, *Studien, 44 n. 1; 116 n. 1.*

rooted like cedars growing at the side of flowing streams. There contending and flourishing in the pursuit of study, masters in public discourse and of learned discussion of the Law, were the distinguished scholars, the genial brothers, my ancestors, the sons of R. Amittai, R. Shephatiah and R. Hananeel, both of them true servants of God, zealously extolling the God of Israel, fervently invoking Him, declaring His praise and holiness: like the company of angels acknowledging the might and dominion of the King of Kings. Among them Aaron established his home. His wisdom streamed forth, his learning flourished there. He revealed great powers, and gave decisions of the law like those which were given when the Urim[1] were in use, when the Sanhedrin held court, and the law of Sota[2] was valid. He extended his influence, he founded a place of study (seat of learning), to take the place of that which had been on the ground of the temple, where the foundations of the ark had been laid. A certain Theophilus committed a sin through criminal intercourse with a married woman.[3] Aaron, before the assembled community, condemned him to death by strangulation. A man laid violent hands on a woman and killed her; the master decided his case with severity, and sentenced him to death by the sword. He then considered the crime of the man who had fallen into idolatry; his case was clear beyond question; he was condemned to death by stoning. Again, a man violated the Law of God, through illicit relations with his mother-in-law; by order of the master the community assembled and put the criminal to death by fire.

By the grace of Him that hath formed the earth by His power, that forgiveth iniquity and sin, I will make mention of the incident that occurred at Venosa. There was a man who had come from the land of Israel, profoundly learned in the law of God, a master of wisdom. He remained there for some time. Every Sabbath he would give instruction and expound the Law before

4b

---

[1] Talmud, *Sota IX 10–48b; Yoma, 21b;* Josephus, *Antiquities III 8, 59.*

[2] The law bearing upon the wife suspected of infidelity (Numbers 5, 11–31) was in force until the time of R. Jochanan ben Zakkai who declared it no longer valid. Mishna, *Sota IX, 9.*

[3] Benny, *The Criminal Code of the Jews, 84ff;* Saalschütz, *Das Mosaische Recht, ch. 58.*

the community of the people of God.   The master would lead
with a discourse on the selected portion of the law, and R.
Silanus[1] would follow with his elucidation.   One day, the men
of the villages came in wagons to the city; they began to quarrel
among themselves.   Some women came out of their houses,
with the long staves used for raking the oven and charred by the
fire; with these the men and women beat one another.   R.
Silanus,[2] in a mistaken spirit of levity, resolved to make use of
the incident, and committed a great wrong.   He sought out the
passage of the scriptural portion that the sage was to expound on
that Sabbath, erased two lines of it and, in their stead, wrote the
story that is told above.   This is what R. Silanus inserted, "The
men came (to the city) in wagons; the women came from their
houses, and beat the men with staves."   On the Sabbath, as the
sage came upon the words, he stopped reading and all speech
failed him.   He looked at the letters and studied, examined and
pondered and went over them several times and finally, in his simplicity, read them, and gave as part of the instruction the words
that he found written there.   Then R. Silanus, in mocking laughter,
said to all assembled there, "Listen to the discourse of the master on
the quarrel that occurred among you yesterday, when the women
beat the men, when they struck them with oven staves and drove
them off on every hand."   When the master realized what had
been done he became very faint, and pale; he hurried to his
associates who were in the school engaged in study, and told them
of the sorrowful experience he had just had.   All of them were
deeply pained and distressed, and they denounced [3] R. Silanus
the wise.[4]

He remained in ban a number of years, until R. Ahimaaz   5a
arrived there on his pilgrimage, and, in his wisdom, annulled
the ban.   This is what the wise man did.   When he arrived,
they were observing the ten days of penitence.   The teachers

[1] The Meturgeman who translated into the vernacular the principal's
reading of the Torah, eventually became, as is indicated, an assistant preacher
or teacher freely using the rabbi's lesson as a text.

[2] Neubauer, *JQR IV*; Kaufmann, *MGWJ 40, 472 note 2*; Ascoli, *Iscrizioni*,
84; Lenormant, *Gazette Archéologique, VIII 208*.

[3] Above, *14*.

[4] Mann, *The Jews of Egypt & Palestine under the Fatim. Caliphs, I 56*.

and head of the school urged him to stand before the ark, and, with ardent devotion, lead them in prayer to Him that is revered in the great assembly of the righteous.

In his modesty, he complied with their request. With the fear of God in his heart, he began with the penitential prayers, then melodiously chanted a poem[1] of R. Silanus to show that he was a man of sound faith; that, although he was at first false and sinful and godless, when he remembered the former teachers, he followed them as his masters, who shattered the power of heretical teachings over him, so that he turned away from the heretics. When the sage had finished the prayers, they asked him who that lover of the great teachers was, so consecrated with power to utter prayer, who loved and honored the masters, and turned away and shunned the heretics. He answered, "That beloved one is R. Silanus, who has been denounced as unworthy among you." They immediately arose and annulled the ban which they had declared against him, and, invoking upon him abundant, enduring and substantial good, all of them said, "May R. Silanus ever be blessed."

In those days a king reigned over the Romans,[2] a wicked man, 5b elevated to the throne through treachery and murder,[3] who determined to make an end of the acknowledgment of the Unity of the Rock whose work is perfect, among the descendants of the

---

[1] In keeping with the custom of the time, permitting the reader of the prayers to insert poems at will, the sage here makes use of a poem of Silanus. The eventual abuse of this freedom, through the addition of the many Piyyutim with their distracting obscurities in word and thought marring the simplicity and solemnity of the service, is denounced by Maimonides (*More 159*); Ibn Ezra, *Kohelet, 5, 1*.

[2] The designation, Romans, is in accord with that which the people and writers of the Byzantine Empire used. In the writings of Cedrenus and Constantine and in the sources generally, they are called Ρωμαιοι. They resented being called Greeks. Latin words, phonetically transcribed, were taken over into the Greek vernacular.

Accounting for the two names by which the Empire was known, Rambaud (*Études sur l'histoire byzantine, 178ff*) says: L'Empire byzantine s'appelait officiellement l'Empire romain bien que le latin à partir du 7e ou du 8e siècle fut passé en Orient à l'état de langue étrangère, de langue morte. Nous l'appelons l'Empire grec parceque l'idiome hellenique était la langue de l'église et de l'état. Finlay, *II. 200;* Freeman, *Historical Essays III, 237ff*.

[3] This brief sketch of Basil reflects accurate knowledge of the treachery by which this Macedonian groom usurped the throne of his master, Michael III.

upright and holy.   In the 800th year after the destruction of the
Holy City and of the Temple, the seat of glory, and of the exile
of the people of Judah and of Israel, there arose a king whose
name was Basil, a worshipper of images,[1] seeking to destroy the
people of Israel[2] ever under God's protection (not widowed), to
lead them astray, to exterminate the remnant of Israel root and
branch, to compel them to abandon the Law and to accept the
worthless doctrine[3] (of Jesus).   He sent couriers and horsemen
to the provinces and all parts of his kingdom, to force the Jews
out of their religion, and make them adopt his senseless faith.
The agents of the king went through the land as far as the harbor
of Otranto; there they embarked and passed over into the province of Apulia.   When the report of their coming reached the
inhabitants, the people were thrown into consternation.   They
traversed the province from end to end.   Finally, they came
to the city of Oria, bringing a letter, officially stamped with the
royal seal,—the seal was the bulla[4] of gold,—that the king had
sent to R. Shephatiah.

And these are the words that were written in the letter, "I,   6a
King Basil, send word to thee R. Shephatiah, to have thee come to
visit me.   Come to me, do not refuse, for I have heard of thy
wisdom and thy vast learning.   I long to see thee; I swear by
my life and by the crown on my head, that thy coming shall be
in peace, and that I will send thee back safe to thy home.   I will
receive thee with honor, as I would one of my own kin, and any
boon thou mayest ask of me, I will grant in grateful affection."

R. Shephatiah then embarked to go to Constantinople, which   6b
Constantine had built—may God shatter its splendor and the

[1] This passage leaves no doubt as to the Emperor Basil who was responsible
for the persecution of the Byzantine Jews.   It is in complete accord with the
tradition of the Byzantine Chroniclers who exalt the founder of the Basilian
dynasty as the defender of the orthodox faith, directing his zeal first against
the "obdurate and recusant" Jews.   Above, 17.

[2] Jeremiah 51, 5.

[3] Krauss, *Studien*, *43 n. 8*.

[4] The seal used exclusively by the Emperor to bestow a boon, even to
suspend, temporarily, the law of the land.   For general official business the
bulla of lead was used.

Eitel, *Ueber Blei- und Gold Bullen im Mittel-Alter*; Sabatier, *Revue
Archéologique XVI 99*; Du Cange, *Glossarium*; Schlumberger, *Sigillographie
de L'Empire byzantine, 8.*

power of all its people.—And God let him find favor in the
presence of the king and of his court.

The king led him into a discussion of the Law, and then ques-   6c
tioned him regarding the building of the Temple, and that of the
church called Sophia,[1] asking him to tell in which structure the
greater wealth had been used. The king firmly contended that
it was Sophia, for in its construction uncounted treasure had been
used. But R. Shephatiah answered, in well-chosen words, "Let
the King command that the Scriptures be brought to him.
There thou wilt find the truth as to which structure is the more
costly." He immediately did so and he found that the quantity
used by David and Solomon was in excess of the amount counted
out for Sophia, by 120 talents of gold and 500 talents of silver.
Thereupon the king exclaimed, "R. Shephatiah, by his wisdom,
has prevailed against me." But R. Shephatiah answered, "My
Lord, not I, but the Scriptures have prevailed against thee."

Then the king asked him to be seated with him at the royal   6d
table, to partake of refreshing delicacies and fruits. Golden
dishes[2] were placed before him that he might eat in the cleanliness
required by the Law. The dishes were drawn up and down by
costly chains of silver, but no one could see the place from
which they were let down before him.

And Basil had a daughter whom he loved as the apple of his   6e
eye. An evil spirit tormented her. He could not find a cure
for her. He spoke to him in secret and with earnest entreaty
said, "Help me, Shephatiah, and cure my daughter of her
affliction"; and Shephatiah answered, "With the help of the
Almighty, I will surely do so." He then asked the king, "Hast

[1] The "Hagia Sophia" at Constantinople, originally built by Constantine,
rebuilt by Theodosius the Younger, and restored by Justinian on a scale of
rare magnificence. Grosvenor, *Constantinople II 494.*

[2] The text is in agreement with all other accounts of the lavish display of
Byzantine royalty. Oriental in origin, this elaborate ceremonial was adopted
and developed by Constantine and his successors "to astonish and overawe
the native and the stranger, to maintain the prestige of the empire; to serve
as a proper setting for the representative of Divinity, set like a statue of gold
upon a mountain, to be worshiped by all the nations of the earth." (Con-
stantin. Porphyr., *De Admin. Imperio, Prooem. 66–67)—De Caeremoniis, ed.
Reiske, 3–5; 516–517;* Ebersolt, *Le Grand Palais de Constantinople et le Livre de
Cérémonies 4ff;* Baudrillart, *Histoire de Luxe Privé et Public, II 331ff.*

thou any secluded place in which there is no uncleanness?"
The king answered: "I have the beautiful garden of the
Bukoleon." [1] After looking about in it, he agreed to make use
of the Bukoleon, which literally means the mouth of the lion.
He took the maiden into it and exorcised the evil spirit in the
name of Him that dwelleth on high, the Creator of height and
depth, that founded the earth in his wisdom, the Maker of the
mountains and seas, that hangeth the world over nothing. The
evil spirit cried out, "Why dost thou help the daughter of the
man who rules in wickedness and heaps affliction upon the
people of the redeemed. She has been delivered to me by God,
that I should humble and crush her. Therefore, let me be, for
I will not come forth from my place." But he answered the evil
spirit, "I will not heed thy words; come forth, in the name of
God, that he may know there is a God in Israel." [2] It came
forth at once and tried to escape; but he seized it and put it into
a leaden chest; he then covered the chest on all sides and sealed
it in the name of his Maker, dropped it into the sea, and let it
sink into the depth of the mighty waters. The maiden, quieted
and cured, then returned to the king and queen.

He now went to the king for his dismissal. The king came   7a
forth to meet him, placed his arm about his neck, brought him
into his chamber, and began to tempt him to abandon his
religion, [3] and, with the promise of large reward, to induce him
to accept the senseless error of his heathen belief. He walked
about with him, and insistently urged him; he approached him
with a bribe and appointed companions for him. When Shephatiah, the master, noticed the fanatic zeal and presumption, he
exclaimed in a loud voice, "Mighty Master, Thou overwhelmest

---

[1] The favorite palace of the Byzantine emperors, built upon the walls along
the Sea of Marmora. Its name was derived from a marble group representing
a lion devouring a bull.

Gyllius, *De Topographia Cple, II 15;* Ville-Hardouin, *La Conquête de
Constantinople, 58;* Van Milligan, *Byzantine Constantinople, 269.*

[2] This is the historical foundation for the popular legend among the Mediaeval
Jews about an eminent sage Shephatiah who had cured the daughter of a
certain King Basil of her possession and had thereby saved five communities
from the persecution in which a thousand were overwhelmed. Graetz (*V, 245,*
refers to it as an unconfirmed tradition. Zunz, *SP 170.*

[3] Above, *18.*

me with violence." Thereupon the king arose from his throne, took him from among the people, and gave him permission to go. He sent him to the queen that she might give him her gift and blessing. And the queen questioned him about his affairs saying, "Hast thou any daughters or sons?" He accordingly answered, "Thy servant has one son and two daughters." She then gave him the rings in her ears and the gird'e on her loins, and urged them upon him, saying, "As my tribute to thy learning, give them to thy two daughters; in costliness there are none to be compared to them." The weight of the rings was a litra of gold and the girdle was of equal value.

When he was about to go, the king again called him and said   7b
to him, "Shephatiah, ask a boon of me and I will give it to thee from my treasures; and if thou dost not desire money I will give thee an inheritance of towns and cities, for I said in my letter to thee, that I would grant thy wish." He answered in sorrow and bitter weeping, "If thou, my Lord, wouldst favor Shephatiah, let there be peace for those engaged in the study of Law. Do not force them to abandon the Law of God, and do not crush them in sorrow and affliction. But if thou be unwilling thus to fulfil my wish, grant for my sake that there be no persecution in my city." The king exclaimed in anger, "Had I not sent a letter with my seal, and taken an oath, I would this very instant punish thee. But how can I harm thee, since I have bound myself in writing to thee, and cannot retract what I have said in my letter." So he issued for him an edict,[1] sealed with a costly seal of gold, commanding that no persecution take place in the city of Oria, and therewith sent him in peace and honor to his home and people.

Then the wicked king continued to send emissaries into all the   7c
provinces and ordered his agents to fall upon them; to force them out of their religion and convert them to the errors and folly of his faith. The sun and moon were darkened for 25 years,[2]

---

[1] Above, *17*.

[2] The word חמש which adds to the difficulty of explaining the chronicle's statement regarding the duration of the persecution, may have been used loosely to complete the rhyme. Kaufmann, *499 note 3*.

until the day of his death. Cursed be his end.[1] May his guilt and wickedness be remembered, and his sin not be forgotten. May the recompense for his vileness and cruelty be visited upon the kingdom of Rome, that his royal power may be cast down from its high places and his dominion be removed from the earth, to bring cheer to the afflicted, and comfort to the mourners, that, in mercy, we may soon see the time of fulfilment.

After his reign, his own son,[2] Leo came to the throne; the   7d
Lord God had chosen him. May his memory be blessed. He annulled the cruel edict that had been enacted in the days of his father, and permitted the Jews to return to the laws and statutes of their religion, to observe their Sabbaths, and all the requirements of their commandments, and the ordinances of their covenant, as of old. Praised be the name of their Rock that did not abandon them in the hands of their enemies, that saved them from their despoilers, and delivered them from their oppressors. Praised be the name of God from the heights forever and ever.

About this time the Arabians[3] began to invade the land with   8a
their armies, to overrun the borders of the kingdom of the uncircumcised, the country of the idolators; they carried destruction into Calabria, threw their cities into confusion, devasted their provinces, razed their walls of defense. They advanced into Apulia; there they grew in power, attacked the inhabitants in force, shattered their strength and captured many cities, and destroyed and plundered.

In those days there was in Bari,[4] Saudan,[5] the chieftain of   8b
the Arabians at the time, who held sway over the entire country.

---

[1] This is the only instance in which the chronicler singles out a Byzantine ruler for bitter remembrance and denunciation.

[2] Above, *19*.

[3] Above, *20*.

[4] The importance of Bari dates from the tenth century when it fell into Byzantine power. Strongly fortified by the Greek emperors, it became the capital of the province of Apulia and the residence of the viceroy. It had long been the principal port of embarkation for pilgrims to the Orient. Taken by the Arabians, it was their base of operations in Italy.

[5] In this account of the Moslem invasions of Italy, the name Saudan is repeatedly used as the nomen proprium of the commander of the garrison at

He sent messengers to the famous city of Oria, to make a treaty
of peace with its inhabitants, promising not to deliver their land
to destruction, only to exact tribute of them. But this was
just a ruse, by which he planned to fall upon the city suddenly
and overthrow it, and lay it waste.

The governor of Bari sent R. Shephatiah to him, to hear his   8c
proposal, to receive his pledge, the document bearing his seal,
that the negotiations might be properly completed with his
official mark. Saudan, the commander, received him with honor,
spoke to him cordially, and lavished attentions upon him in the
presence of all the princes that had assembled to welcome him;
and he detained him until it was almost Sabbath. He did it
purposely; for he could not return to his city on the Sabbath.
He would not let him go, so that he might not inform his master
of the enemy's plans. When R. Shephatiah became aware of his
ruse he exclaimed, "Give me permission to go, for thou hast
deceived me with thy cunning. But Saudan answered, "Whither
wilt thou go at this hour, the Sabbath is about to begin." Again
he said to him, "Let me go, my lord, do not be concerned about
me." So he permitted him to leave, and he went. And when
he set out, invoking the help of the Almighty, trusting in the
Name of his Creator, and confident that God would aid him, he
wrote some letters on the horse's hoof, so that his journey might
be quickly made; he rapidly repeated the Ineffable Name and
the ground miraculously yielded before him.

And when he reached the outskirts of his city, he called to   8d
the people on every hand, "Come forth in haste; flee from the
outer city, for Saudan, the commander of the Arabians, with all
his forces, is coming to take our possessions, to kill, to rob and
plunder." And as he drew near the governor of the city went out
to meet him; R. Shephatiah told him what had happened to
him, and they took counsel about the matter. So he arrived
in the city before nightfall; he washed and bathed, and welcomed

Bari. It is probably a title, designating the officer's rank, a Hebrew adapta-
tion of σολδανος, soldanus and saogdan of the chronicles of the period.

Kaufmann, *502 n. 1*; C. Famin, *Hist. d. Invasions Sarrasins en Italie*
(7–11s) 399.

the Sabbath as was fitting, with rejoicing, with food and drink, with study of the Law, robed and adorned in festive garments, partaking of all its delights and at ease among them.

And Saudan and all his host, arrogant and insolent, came by 8e forced marches to attack them. He found the country deserted to the very gates of the city; and on the Sabbath, at the time of the afternoon prayer, having found no satisfaction, he asked for R. Shephatiah, saying, "Give me the man who violated his law, and profaned his Sabbath; their law ordains that he be put to death." And R. Shephatiah answered fearlessly, by the power of his God that was in him, "Why dost thou speak thus? There is no truth in thy words. My witness is in heaven, and all the people of my city can testify that I arrived while it was day; while the sun was up I returned and went to the bath; I washed and bathed and returned to my house, and welcomed the Sabbath with proper sanctification, in obedience to the command of my King and my Redeemer, the Holy One of Israel, my God."

And Abu Aaron, the Aaron mentioned before, was still in the 9a city at the time; he had come to the city of Bari situated on the seacoast, built facing the sea; and Saudan came forth to meet him and bestowed great honor upon him. Aaron remained with him about six months. Saudan's love of him was more wonderful than the love of women. While he remained with him, Saudan did not swerve from his good counsel. Aaron informed him clearly on everything that he asked of him, as though he were consulting the Urim. The wisdom of his instruction was acknowledged during all the time he remained there.

But one day as Aaron awoke from sleep, the spirit of God 9b began to urge him to return to his native land. He went to the seacoast and looked about and found a ship ready to sail for Egypt. He immediately embarked upon it. The ship began to move at great speed. In anguish Saudan sent out ships to overtake it; but the master, by the power of the Great Hand, uttered the Name, and the ships could not approach it. The sailors tried to return to the place from which they had set sail, but the ship could not reach the shore. When the commander saw this, his anger subsided, for he perceived and understood that miracles were being performed by the master's power.

Thereupon the commander exclaimed, "O my master, my master; my father, my father! my horsemen and my chariots, why hast thou left and forsaken me? Accept my prayer, return my lord, take my wealth and treasures, do not leave me alone!" Aaron fittingly answered, "My way is plainly ordained by Him that excelleth in power; I cannot change it. Inquire of me and I will tell thee what thou desirest to know, before I leave thee." So he questioned him about many things, and Aaron gave answer in keeping with his questions. Finally he asked, "Will I enter Beneventum?" And Aaron answered, "Thou wilt enter; not in joy, but through sad compulsion." As he foretold, so it happened. And Aaron went rejoicing to the quiet of the inheritance which he had left in his native land; he reached his home to live in abundance and content, in prosperity and joy, and gave thanks and praise to his Guardian and Creator that had brought him back, safe and happy, to his home. 9c

I will now proceed to tell of the wonderful things that were done by R. Hananeel. He had a cousin, named Papoleon, who died very young. On the day of his death, the brothers of R. Hananeel were away at Beneventum on business. So he delayed burying him in the tomb of his fathers, waiting for his brothers to come and weep over their dead kinsman and to give him proper burial. To prevent the body from decomposing and becoming putrid, he wrote upon a piece of parchment the Name of God, his Master, and placed the parchment under the dead man's tongue. The Name brought him to life, and raised him, and he sat up in bed. He repeated the Name, and gazed at it. During the night preceding the day on which the brothers returned, they had an astonishing dream: an angel of God seemed to come in a vision and speak the mysterious words, "Why do you vex the Lord God, and do things which are not right? God putteth to death and you bring to life. You should not do so. You should not tempt the Lord your God." But they did not know what R. Hananeel had done. When they reached their house he came out to meet them; they went in to see their 9d

cousin and found him sitting on his bed; they knew nothing of
what had occurred, of the Name (that was) under his tongue.
When they heard what had been done, they wept bitterly and
said to their brother, "Thou wast able to bring him to life, and
thou canst put him to death." In sadness and anguish R.
Hananeel then approached his cousin and said, "Raise thy
mouth, that I may kiss thee." The boy opened his mouth. R.
Hananeel, kissing him, put his hand under his tongue, and took
therefrom the Name written on the parchment. As soon as
the Name was taken from him, his body fell back upon the bed.
So the body returned to dust and decay, and the soul returned
to God who gave it.

I will give thanks to God and declare His works, and speak of   10
that which should be told, which happened in the city of Oria in
the palace called Hegemonia, to R. Hananeel, the brother of
Shephatiah, who was on the verge of death, and whom the
Exalted One brought forth to deliverance, from darkness to
light. It is the duty of his descendants, heirs (pillars) of nobility,
to give praise and grateful recognition to his Name, and at all
times say before Him Hallelujah.

One day the archbishop[1] questioned him regarding various   10
matters recorded in the official archives, and eventually entered
into discussion[2] of the calculations that were prescribed for
determining the appearance of the new moon. On the morrow
of that very day there was to be New Moon day, which, according
to Israel's custom, was to be held sacred. He asked him in how
many hours the new moon would appear. R. Hananeel answered
by naming a certain hour. But he was mistaken. The archbishop disputed his opinion and said, "If that is thy calculation
on the appearance of the moon, thou are not skilled in calculation." R. Hananeel had not given thought to the time of the
appearance of the New Moon, but the archbishop had calculated
it and knew; he had cast his net for R. Hananeel, and would

---

[1] The designation ἡγεμων, originally that of a military or political leader,
was later applied to the primate of the Greek Church. Gay, *Les Higoumènes*,
284; Krauss, *Studien, 105 n. 3, 4.*

[2] Graetz, *V 229*; Güdemann, II *12, 24, 37, 39, 230*; Kohler, *Disputations*,
JE IV 614.

have caught him in his snare had not the God of his salvation come to his aid. And the archbishop said to him, "O wise Hananeel, if the new moon appear as I have calculated, thou shalt do my will and adopt my religion, as my gospel teaches, abandon thy faith, and the ordinances of thy law, and accept my religion, my empty doctrine of error. If it be as thou hast calculated, I will do thy will. I will give thee my horse, assigned to me at the (ceremonies of) New Year's day, the value of which is 300 pieces of gold; and if thou care not for the horse, thou mayest take its value instead." They accepted the conditions, and agreed to abide by what they had spoken, before judges and magistrates and before the prince that ruled over them. That night the archbishop ordered men to go to the top of the wall and towers, to note the exact moment of the moon's first appearance, and observe the portion that appeared.

When R. Hananeel returned to his house, he went over his calculation and found his error, by which he had failed in his reckoning; his heart grew faint and melted within him, no strength was left in him. But he roused himself to entreat God and His favor, the Ancient Help, from the beginning of time, to show His marvelous power in his need, to lift him from the walls of the pit. He went to his brothers and all of his kin and told them of the trouble that had come upon him, that they might make earnest supplication to God; perhaps He would hear their cry, and would intervene with all his signs and wonders, as He had marvelously done in Egypt for his forefathers. When it grew dark, he went to the roof of his house, looking to Him on high, to whom praise and exaltation are due. As the time of waxing approached, and the moon was about to shine, he called, in distress and tears, upon Him that heareth the supplication of His beloved, saying, in his prayers to the God of his hope, "O God, Ruler of the universe, nothing is hidden from thee, my thoughts are revealed to Thee. I have not been presumptuous; I have innocently erred and committed folly. And now, O God of my praise, may my prayer come before Thee; arise, to help me, O God of my salvation; forgive my error and pardon my wrong doing, so that I shall not suffer punishment; else my

11a

death is better than my life.   Do not destroy the work of Thy
hands, and do not withdraw Thy kindness from Thy servant;
overlook the transgression according to Thy measure of grace
and mercy; in Thy great goodness pardon my iniquity; give ear
to my prayer and supplication; accept my plea and cry of affliction; hear my entreaty for Thy sake, O God, and I will extol
Thee in the assembly of the elders, and give homage to Thee
in the company of the upright."

And He that is enthroned amid the praises (of Israel) heard   11
his prayer. The moon was obscured and did not appear until
the next night. In the morning he went to hear the decision;
the archbishop summoned him in the presence of all the people,
and said to him, "Thou knowest as well as I that the new moon
appeared as I had determined in my calculations; I was not
mistaken; I had given much thought to it, and knew I had the
correct answer. But who can inflict punishment on thee? Thou
hast found exemption from thy Master like a son that escapes
punishment by caressing and coaxing his father." So he gave
him the 300 pieces of gold. R. Hananeel distributed them among
the poor and did not take any of the money to his own house.
Then his brothers and friends assembled and gave praise and
thanks to the Eternal One, that saveth His servants from
affliction, and bringeth them from darkness to light, at all times
their Help, mercifully sustaining His people with shield and
place of refuge.

I will now return to the incident of which I have above written   1
in part, regarding Theophilus who fell by his sin, and who was
condemned to death by strangulation. As he went out to be
executed all the people gathered about him at the sound of his
bitter outcry. The governor of the city came upon them and
drove off the multitude and said to the man, "If thou wilt
abandon thy religion and truly adopt mine, I will save thee from
an unnatural death." He nodded approval, for he yearned to
save himself. The ruler at once had him taken to his palace.
But upon questioning him, he found him loyal to the religion of
the Hebrews. He then said to him, "I helped thee and took
thee from the hands of the executioners, but thou hast lied to me

and mocked at me. I will punish thee with severity and with cruelty, with horrible torture." He began to strike him, to beat him with fiendish blows; he cut off his hands and his feet, and cast him into prison and confined him there.

There was another Jew in prison with him, a God-fearing man, who brought him food and drink every day. When none was set aside for him, he would give him some of his own; he himself looked after him until an entire year had passed. And on the eve of the Day of Atonement, on which the people of God makes atonement for its sins, this Jew brought food and drink to him and ate with him. And Theophilus had a young daughter. He said to his companion, "Go bring witnesses, for I wish to give her in marriage to thee." He answered, "My Lord, thou art a man of distinction and I am one of the lowly; if thy kinsmen hear of this, they will tear me to pieces like a fish." [1] But he said, "No man rules in my house; no one, no member of my family has authority over my daughter; she is in my power alone." He went forth and found three witnesses, and before them Theophilus offered his daughter in marriage. Then he said, "Go in peace; hereafter thou wilt not again find me." After the festival this man returned to look for him in the prison house, but he did not find him, alive or dead, for God had taken him. May God forgive his iniquity, pardon all his sins; may his soul rest in His realm of bliss.

R. Shephatiah was once walking about the streets of the city 12a at night, and he heard the sound of wailing in the house of a neighbor and friend; he heard one woman speaking to another, the one above saying to her companion below, "Sister, take the child and keep him and together we will eat him." He listened closely to her words; he immediately went in and took the child from her. Those women were not daughters of men, but demons who were passing in the night.[2] He brought the child to his home, and showed him to his wife. They recognized him and concealed him in his bedroom. The child's father and mother

[1] Talmud, *Pesahim, 47;* Dembitz, *Services, 27.*

[2] The Chronicle truly reflects the belief prevailing throughout the mediaeval world that demons were ever seeking to prey upon men. Michelet, *La Sorcière.*

7

had passed the entire night in anguish and in bitter weeping and lamentation, and in the morning had taken him out to the grave-yard to bury him. As they were returning from the place of burial to their home, R. Shephatiah came to see them, after the custom of those who comfort mourners, and questioned them about their son, as to what sickness he had had, and what affliction had taken him off. They replied, "O master, he sat with us until evening; he ate at the table with us; we retired to our beds; when we awoke from our sleep we found him lying dead among us. All night we wept, in sorrow and anguish, and read the prayers for the dead, and in the morning we went out to bury him in his grave, by the side of his fathers." Thereupon R. Shephatiah, to console them, answered, "I must tell you that I cannot agree with what you say; take me to the grave in which you have buried him; for your son is not in the grave, he is still alive; I will bring him to your house, and, with the help of God, will deliver him alive and well." So they went to the grave and looked about, but they found nothing but a broom, such as is used in sweeping the house. R. Shephatiah then returned to his house with them; he told them all that had happened, and restored the child to them. And they praised Him that heareth prayer, that heareth (the cry of) the Jews, that ruleth over the wind.

R. Shephatiah had a daughter named Cassia, of rare beauty, 12ᵇ of genial and charming disposition, and he loved her devotedly. Her father wished to have her marry but her mother did not wish it. Whenever anyone came (sent) to ask her in marriage, her mother would turn him away by saying, "My daughter is a woman of high station, and her father is a distinguished man; if we do not find one like him, I will not let her come out of the house. If there be one like her father in mastery of the Law, of tradition and scripture, in the interpretation of Talmudic prac-tice and in the knowledge of decisions, in the understanding of Sifri and Sifra, in ability to explain and apply the principle of major and minor, in familiarity with the mysteries of Binah and Hokmah,[1] and all secret lore, in wealth and eminence, in influence

[1] Dembitz, *Services*, 50ff.

and authority, in his grasp of the statutes and commandments, in reverence and modesty, if he have every good quality, (I will give her in marriage to him, as we should)."

One night, while R. Shephatiah was about to recite his prayers 12c —as was his custom to pray, declaring the power of the Eternal, chanting songs of praise and sanctification, making entreaty to God, with psalms exalting and seeking the refuge of the shadow of the Almighty, with tuneful melody invoking Him that rideth upon the clouds, finding strength and security before the throne of His enduring might, trusting and resting in the Lord that dwelleth above, magnifying Him whose majesty is in the heavens, that laid the foundation of the earth by commandments and statutes, that spread out the heavens by ordinances of joy, that established the firmament by the Everlasting Law; Him, whose voice is mighty upon the waters, whose glory is above the heavens, 12d —it happened that his daughter arose from her bed, and, in her sleeping gown, stood before him, to pour the water for him, that he might wash his hands; he noticed that she had arrived at the time of maturity for marriage. At the conclusion of his prayer, he returned to his wife, to rebuke her, to shame her, to emphasize the truth of his words, saying with great vehemence, "I have a precious dove, without blemish. She has arrived at maturity to be a crown to her husband, and my brother seeks her in marriage for his son Hasadiah. I have followed your advice and have not found happiness for her; I have violated the ordinance of the Scriptures and disregarded the words of the sages." [1] The next morning as he was leaving his house to go to the house of prayer, he called to his brother R. Hananeel. He quickly came to him and heard him say, "It is my intention and earnest desire to give my daughter to Hasadiah thy son, for it is best that I give her to him." And R. Hananeel in extreme modesty fell on his knees before him. When they concluded their prayers, he invited the congregation to come to his house, and gave his daughter in marriage to R. Hasadiah, son of R. Hananeel the brother of R. Shephatiah. R. Amittai, the brother of the distinguished bride, wrote, in her honor, the poem, "The Lord

[1] Mishna, *Aboth V 13;* Mielziner, *Jewish Law of Marriage and Divorce,* 71.

that from the beginning telleth the end," to crown her with charm
and beauty, when this bride and groom were united in marriage.

R. Shephatiah had grown old;[1] God had blessed him with all 13a
good qualities; He that dwelleth on high had endowed him with
learning, distinguished him with wealth and large possessions;
and had favored him with a worthy, upright son; father and son
were without fault. And R. Hananeel was equal to them in
eminence and uprightness. They were ever moved by the fear of
God, brothers and devoted comrades, gracious in friendship, at all
times engaged in the study of the law and the commandments,
eagerly observing the ordinances of God, zealously extolling the
power and splendor of their King, earnestly declaring the honor
and majesty of their Master, exalting their Creator with precious
crown and diadem; acknowledging their Maker's might, evening
and morning, in the assembly for prayer. All the days of their
life they sorrowfully bewailed the captivity and the destruction
of the Temple; they lamented the persecution in bitter anguish
as long as they lived; they invoked Him that turneth backward the wise, and entreated Him by whose wisdom the depths
are laid open; that hath set bounds for the rivers and seas, that
He might confound the plans of the enemy, and destroy his
kingdom; they prayed to Him that aboundeth in mercy, for
understanding, that He might defeat and annul the edict of
persecution. Through their supplication to the Most Exalted,
the decree was not carried out beyond the other side of the sea.
He saved His servants devoted to His laws, from contamination
(filth) and corruption, and from the loathsome waters (of baptism); from the enforced worship of the deaf and dumb, and
from adoration of the blind: from the worship of idols. He
roared against their foes with the voice of the thunder; He
visited His wrath upon their enemies and persecutors, and
delivered His beloved ones from the power of their foes; He
rescued their souls from the raging fire, so that they might be
eagerly devoted to the Law, and might relish the odor (fragrance)
of the spices and perfumes that have of old been stored and
sealed in the treasure houses of Eden.—R. Shephatiah died in

---

[1] Halper, *Post-Bibl. Lit. II*, 96.

peace; he closed his life in happy devotion to the Judge of the widow and the Father of the orphan; leader among the wise, he tasted of the cup of the first parents, which the first serpent brought upon the first and last generations.[1]

On New Year's day R. Shephatiah alone was thought worthy 13b of the honor of sounding the Shofar, for the glory of God through His people. On that day he was weak, prostrated by sickness. But the whole congregation urged him insistently, saying: "Our master, arrayed in light, the radiance of our glory, the light of our eyes, blow the Shofar for us; as long as God spares you, no one else shall blow the Shofar for us." They continued to urge him and he arose to blow it. But he did not have sufficient strength and could not produce the proper sounds. The good man calmly accepting the judgment against him said to them, "My children, may this be a sign for good unto you; because of my transgression time has turned against me." He left the house of worship and went to his home and lay upon his bed. The entire congregation followed him and entered his bedchamber. Turning his face to them, he said, "I am going to my eternal rest, to my portion among the fathers of old, and I tell you dear children, my three beloved sons, that Basil the oppressor and persecutor is dead. He passes on before me, bound in chains of fire, delivered to the demons of destruction. My God, whose name is the Lord of Hosts, has sent me to go forth to meet Basil and to stand in judgment against him, for all the evil that he has committed against His people, to blot out his name and the name of his posterity, to destroy him root and branch." So they noted the day and hour. Soon afterward the report reached them, announcing that Basil the oppressor had died; the letter came just as the good man had foretold. It was the custom of the emperors of Constantinople, whenever an emperor died, to make proclamation by letter, in Bari, giving the day and the time when he had passed away. "Praised be He

[1] The author is not to be held too strictly to his initial promise of an orderly presentation of the family traditions. Here, with the story of this ancestor's death, having led us to believe that he has made use of all the material relating to him, he loosely appends other traditions that he seems hitherto to have overlooked.

who alone doeth wonders, who destroyed him in this world and shut him out of the world to come. Praised be His name and the name of His glory. I shall be gathered to my people and shall go to my place and as for you my children, my devoted ones, the assembly of my people, may God be with you,—He that dispenseth death and life, I am that I am, reviving the faithful children of Benjamin and the lion's whelp (Judah)."

After the death of Shephatiah, who had served God without de- 14a
ceit, and, with constant devotion, studied the mysteries of the Highest, faithfully loved the Lord and obeyed Him with all his soul and might, and, with all his heart, had magnified Him, there arose R. Amittai[1] his beloved son, who eagerly adhered to the ways of 14b
his father, and did not stray from the statutes of his Creator. The God of his father was his help. He continued his school, to promote, with the sages of his company (circle), the study of the law of God. The day before he died, his father had demanded this of him, that he should maintain the assembly of teachers, and direct it properly, so that the teachers and pupils might not be disbanded. He held the assembly together, carried on instruction with the help of the rabbis and sages, and expounded the Torah, systematically, in its length and breadth; his principles of interpretation of the Commandments of God and His covenant were those of his ancestors. His soul lamented the destruction of the Temple, and grieved deeply over the persecution, so long as he lived.

One day he went out to his vineyard, his estate beyond the 14c
limits of the city. On that day a stranger, a wise man and true servant of God, had died. And the elders of the community sent word to him asking him to come and join them in doing their duty to the dead, to mourn for him and bury him, to show the respect enjoined by the Law.[2] He said to them in reply: "Come to me, beyond the limits of the city; I will wait for you and go

---

[1] The former nebulous figure of this prolific writer of synagogal poetry is here brought into clear relief. The authorities had doubtfully assigned him to the time of the destruction of the first Temple and again, to the close of the eleventh century, after the first Crusade.

Kaufmann, *506*; Landshuth, *46*;

Zunz, *Lit. 106, 166, S. P. 185.*

[2] Schulchan Aruch, *Yore Dea 374.*

with you to the place of burial, and will recite the prescribed prayers for the dead." The entire community came out to bury the man. R. Amittai conducted the burial service for him, and all the people in lamentation wept for him; R. Amittai lamented him in a dirge which he had especially composed for him. This is the beginning of the poem in which he mourned him, "O hospitality, O exile! they that do not know Thee, make sport of Thee; they that confess Thee, cry out in sorrow." His brother, R. Moses, a teacher of children, was there; he sneeringly whispered to the bystanders, "They that confess and know Thee, are overwhelmed with afflictions." R. Amittai heard him; and ever after he kept in mind the offense of that teacher. A long while afterward, a married woman was suspected of sin, and the community met to investigate her conduct and pronounce judgment; they found no witness against the woman except R. Moses, the teacher of children; there was no one to testify with him. R. Amittai then said to him, in accordance with the law, "Hast thou another witness, as the Torah requires?" But no other witness appeared with him. Thereupon he ordered the clerk to put him in ban. He pronounced judgment against him as ordained in the Law, visited his own device upon him, compelled him to leave Oria, and sent him into exile. He went to the city of Capua, and from there journeyed to Pavia.[1]

R. Amittai was gathered to his people. He left a son named Abdiel. And Abdiel had a son whose name was Baruch, who was not learned in the Law as his fathers had been. In the days of Baruch there was in his house a copy of the Sefer Merkaba which R. Shephatiah had used all his life. One day, on the eve of the Sabbath, on which God rested from all His work, as the day grew dark, and as there was no one to kindle the light before the Sefer Merkaba, a woman, defiled through her uncleanness, —may she be blotted from the book of life, and kept out of the world to come—came up to kindle the light before the Torah.

15a

---

[1] It is suggested by Kaufmann (508) that this may be the Moses of Pavia, who through a few imperfect references, is regarded as one of the early masters of Talmud study among the Jews of Italy.

Zunz, *SP 19*; Halberstam, in Kohut, *Aruch I. 38*; Güdemann, *Die Juden in Italien, 14 note 3.*

And the wrath of God fell upon that family; many died of the plague, only a few remained. And there was a wise Jew among them, who saw the meaning of the visitation. He seized the book, put it into a leaden case and cast it into the deep waters. The sea receded almost a mile. After he had thrown the case into the sea, the waters returned within their bounds; the evil decree was immediately annulled, and the plague was stayed. But the memory of Baruch perished, his lamp was extinguished; so that he left no one to engage in the study of the Law; he had no sons; only one daughter.

R. Hasadiah, son of R. Hananeel, had a son whose name was   15b
Paltiel. And R. Paltiel begat a son, R. Hananeel, and a daughter, Cassia who was distinguished for piety; she begat a son, R. Paltiel, who was a master of astrology.

In those days the Arabians with their armies, with Al Muizz   15c
as their commander,[1] overran Italy; they devastated the entire province of Calabria, and reached Oria, on the border of Apulia; they besieged it, defeated all its forces; so that the city was in dire distress; its defenders had no power to resist; it was taken by storm; the sword smote it to the very soul. They killed most of its inhabitants, and led the survivors into captivity. And the commander inquired about the family of R. Shephatiah.[2] He sent for them and had them appear before him. And God let them find grace in his eyes. He bestowed His kindness upon R. Paltiel, His servant, and let him have favor before him. And Al Muizz brought him to his tent, and kept him at his side, to retain him in his service.

One night the commander and R. Paltiel went out to observe   15d
the stars. As they were gazing at them, they saw the commander's star consume three stars, not all at one time, but in succession. And Al Muizz said to him, "What meaning dost

[1] The word קייט, designating the Arabian commander of the garrison at Bari, is a hebraized form of Caytus, Caetus, &c. of the Greek and Latin sources. Kaufmann, (*ZDMG 51, 436*) derives it from *Ka'id*, as suggested by Heinemann (*Geschichte der Normannen, I, 28.*).

Du Cange, *Glossarium;* Lupus Protospatarius, Migne *PL 155, 23 note 15; 131.*

[2] Above, *21.*

thou find in that?" R. Paltiel answered "Give thy interpretation first." The commander replied, "The stars represent the
three cities, Tarentum, Otranto and Bari, that I am to conquer."
R. Paltiel then said, "Not that, my Lord; I see something
greater; the first star means that thou wilt rule over Sicily;
the second, that thou wilt rule over Africa, and the third, that
thou wilt rule over Babylonia."[1] Al Muizz at once embraced
him and kissed him, took off his ring and gave it to him, and
took an oath saying, "If thy words come true, thou shalt be
master of my house and have authority over all my kingdom."

Before seven days had passed, a message was brought to Al 16a
Muizz. The princes of Sicily[2] sent messengers to him saying,
"Know that the Emir is dead. Come thou in haste and assume
authority and dominion over us." He thereupon gathered his
troops; with all the captains of his army he embarked on his
ships and crossed over into their country, and became their
ruler. Then he had faith in the words of R. Paltiel, and did not
depart from his advice, either to the left or to the right; he
appointed him master over his house and domain. He (R.
Paltiel) entered his service as his vizier.

Some time after, Al Muizz went to Ifrikiya, leaving his brother 16b
as ruler over Sicily; and R. Paltiel went with him. There he
grew in eminence, and added to his fame; he was second in
power to the Caliph,[3] his renown spread through all the cities.

At that time, the emperor[4] of Greece sent an embassy with a gift 16c

[1] The name of the third conquest has been variously interpreted. In the
opinion of Bacher it refers simply to Bologna. Such, at first, was also the view
of Kaufmann, remarking that in the light of subsequent history Egypt must
have been intended. Later (ZDMG 51,), he finds support for this interpretation through the aid of D. H. Muller and Goldziher who show that Babylonia
was frequently used for Cairo and thus for Egypt as a whole.

Ville-Hardouin makes use of the phrase 'Babylone d'Egypte' with the
explanatory remark, 'Aujourd'hui Caire.' (Histoire de la Conquête de Cple.,
282).

[2] Above, 23; Quatremère, Jour. As. 1837, 207.

[3] Above, 25.

[4] The author has the one term מֶלֶךְ for the titles of eminent authority.
Emperor, Governor, Commander, Caliph, &c.

The text freely employs the words Roman, Greek and Macedonian as
equivalents of Byzantine. The same interchange of these denominations is
found in the Khazar document edited by Schechter, JQR, N. S. III 194 note 22.

to seek audience with the Caliph of Ifrikiya. The ambassador came in state as was the custom of the Greeks. He asked who was warden of the palace and master of the royal ceremonies. An Arabian said to him, "It is a Jew that gives permission to enter and leave; he is in authority over all the Caliph's dominion; and the Caliph always follows his advice. No one can see him or enter the palace to appear before him without the order and consent of the Jew." But the Greek, in his insolence and pride, in his folly and stupidity, replied, "I would rather leave this city and return to Constantinople, to my master who has sent me hither, than deal with the Jew for permission to let me speak to the Caliph." These words reached the ear of R. Paltiel; he was informed of all that had occurred. He then commanded throughout the royal court that no one approach him (the envoy) with a sign of greeting or respect, and that no one take notice of him where he had set up his tent. For about ten days he kept aloof, in anger and raging fury. Then, he meekly came up to ask mercy and pardon, begging that he forget his senseless conduct, and forgive the offense which he had committed in his stupidity, and the words he had spoken in his folly. R. Paltiel granted that he might come, but not on that day. On the third day, he admitted him into his presence; he received him with honor and splendor, and overwhelmed him with lavish gifts, entertained him with music, and dances, and an abundance of perfumes, with precious stones, onyx and opal, and with the costly and beautiful treasures of the realm. He received him in state, from the gate of his palace, to his dining hall; he adorned the entire hall with hangings of silk and wool; the floor of the court and the walls of the palace were beautified with tapestry of scarlet and fine linen and costly ornaments; he walked in upon rugs of silk. The Greek saw R. Paltiel sitting upon a couch, and, for himself, he found a chair of gold. He took his seat and entered into conversation with him, questioned him about the law of the Hebrews, about his kin, and family and native land; R. Paltiel answered him properly and intelligently. And he gave order that water be brought to wash his hands and mouth, in a dish and bowl of onyx and jasper. Secretly he commanded the

servant to break them, after he had washed. The servant [1]
carried out the command of his master; he brought the bowl,
and its dish; he poured the water over his master's hands, and
then fell at his feet, and broke the dishes. Thereupon the Greek
arose in amazement and grew pale. But R. Paltiel laughingly
turned to him and said before all gathered about him, "Why art
thou disturbed; why dost thou rise from thy seat in amazement?" The Greek envoy replied, "Because I have seen great
damage done. There is no way of replacing the priceless bowl
and dish that have been broken." R. Paltiel then questioned
him about the king of the Greeks, as to whether dishes of gold
or of precious stone were used in his palace, and the Macedonian
ambassador said, "Dishes of gold are used in my master's house."
To which R. Paltiel replied, "Thy master is a man of limited
means. Dishes of precious stones and gems are more costly
than dishes of gold; for those that are made of precious stone,
cannot be restored when broken, but those of gold, when dam-
aged, can be mended without loss; many dishes of rare stone and
gems such as thou hast just seen broken in my house, are broken
in the palace of my master, the Caliph." Thereupon he dismissed
him with honor, to the king of Greece who had sent him.

R. Hananeel, the son of Paltiel, asked permission[2] of the Caliph 17a
of Ifrikiya to cross the sea and go to Italy, for at the time of the
captivity of Oria, those that were spared sought refuge in Bari
and Otranto, bringing their household goods with them, and
saving the money of others with their own. So R. Hananeel
went to Constantinople, and, sorely depressed and afflicted,
entreated the King to receive him with favor, to grant him the
authority, under royal seal, to travel through all cities of his
kingdom and, with his will and consent, enter any place in which
he might find property belonging to him. He took the sealed
letter of authority and went to the city of Bari. There he found
an old copy of the Scriptures that had been his, and ornaments
of the clothes of women, and sewed garments that they wore.

[1] Above, 24.

[2] A Jewish master of astrology was immune from the persecution that
the mass of his coreligionists suffered, and had unquestioned access to the
royal presence. Lacroix, *Science and Lit. in the M. A.*, 211.

8

The teachers and sages[1] of Bari disputed their possession with
him, in accordance with the principle[2] that he who saves anything
from an invading army, from the water or the fire, may claim it
as his own; for this was the teaching of Rab, in the interpretation
of the Mishna. He replied, "It is as you say, but our sages
have also taught that 'the law of the land is the binding law';[3]
here is the written edict with the seal, which the Emperor issued
for me." So they divided with him. They gave him the robes
and the copy of the Scriptures, and he left them the remainder
as a compromise. He went down to Beneventum and the entire
community respectfully welcomed him. He remained there an
entire year. Then he made his home there, and married one of
its women, Esther, daughter of R. Shabbethai, of the family
of R. Amittai. In His mercy He turned in kindness, and bestowed His compassion and visited His favor and truth upon the
house of R. Shephatiah and R. Hananeel, men of His choice,
who, serving Him as long as they lived, did not stray from his law.
For it is His promise to do good to those who look to His salvation and wait for His help. He favored him in his old age with
worthy sons, R. Samuel, his first born, the beginning of his
strength, and R. Shabbethai,[4] and Papoleon, and Hasadiah.
Hasadiah went to Ifrikiya with R. Paltiel, the son of his sister

[1] As in all the sources bearing upon this period of the history of the Jews in
Italy, the Chronicle maintains the accepted tradition regarding the eminence
of the sages of Bari. Graetz, (VI 259) however, denies them this distinction
and finds nothing more than meaningless praise in all such tributes as that
contained in the current proverb, "from Bari goeth forth the Law, and the
word of the Lord from Otranto" (quoted by Rabbenu Tam—latter half of
twelfth century—in his principal work, *Sefer ha-Yashar, 74a*).
E. N. Adler, *REJ 67, 40;* Güdemann *II 17*.

[2] A principle upheld by the authority of Rab (Abba Arika, d. 247) was
generally followed as final. As a distinguished pupil of Judah ha-Nasi and
founder of the Academy of Sura, who elevated Babylonian Jewry to a place
of leadership which it held for several centuries, his interpretation of the Law
was accepted as binding. "He found the Law an open, neglected field and
fenced it in." (Talmud, *Hulin 110a*).

[3] An ordinance of Samuel, master of the Academy of Nehardea (165–257).
He was the leading authority of Babylon in civil law.
Talmud, *Gittin 10b, Baba K., 113a,* Mielziner, *Introduction to the Talmud,*
44; Reinach, *Histoire 45*.

[4] Krauss, *Studien, 87 n. 5*.

Cassia. R. Samuel came to the city of Capua and there married a woman named Albavera. Some time after, R. Shabbethai and Papoleon set out with the gift which was sent by the prince of Amalfi to R. Paltiel. After the manner of young men, they entered into conversation with the pilot of the ship, and said, "Let us write the Name, so that we may move at great speed, and reach the coast of Ifrikiya tonight." So they wrote and pronounced the Name of Him that dwelleth on High, and cast the writing into the waters, and they said to the sailors, "Keep very close watch on us, that we do not fall asleep." But their sin brought calamity upon them and deep sleep fell upon them; a storm wind tossed them about on the water; the ship capsized and the men sank in deep waters. The power of the Name took the ship to Spain and Narbonne and to the sea of Constantinople; then brought it back to the sea of Ancona, and finally wrecked it before the city of Amalfi.

Upon the death of the ruler of Egypt, the elders of Egypt,   18a through reliable couriers, wise and chosen messengers, sent a letter authorized by the princes and nobles and the people of the cities and villages to Al Muizz, Caliph of the Arabians,[1] in which they said "We have heard of thy mighty deeds, the violence of thy wars, which thou hast waged in thy wisdom, of thy sagacity in which thou excellest the princes that formerly ruled over the kingdom of Syene[2] (Egypt). Now, come to us, be king over us, with the consent of our princes and all the eminent men of our country; we will be thy subjects, thou shalt be our king."

He considered the proposal; R. Paltiel was summoned; and   18b they took counsel together as to what they should do, for it was a long journey, through a barren and desolate land; all the way there was no water; no supplies of food; no tents or places of shelter. R. Paltiel set out in advance and established the camps; he erected bazaars and places for lodging, appointed merchants for them, and supplied them with bread, water, fish, meat, garden produce, and everything necessary for soldiers coming from the distant cities. Then the Caliph and princes

[1] Above, *23*.
[2] Ezekiel 29, 10.

and courtiers set out; they pitched the tents of their encampment
three miles from Egypt (Cairo).   All the nobles of Egypt joyfully
came forth to greet them, their chiefs and governors, their
officials and princes and the masses of the people as well.   They
came up to him and prostrated themselves.   He made them take
an oath of allegiance, by their law, and accepted their hostages,
princes of the people.   Then R. Paltiel entered Egypt with a
division of the forces, detailed them on the walls and towers,
that they might guard the city, the palace and public buildings,
and appointed sentinels to be on guard, day and night, on the
outskirts and the borders.   And then the Caliph with all his army
marched in.   The nobles and all the people gathered about him,
and again swore allegiance to him.   He walked into the court
and took his seat in his palace, on the throne of his dominion
and majesty.   They put the sceptre into his hand, and the royal
crown upon his head, and he reigned over the kingdom of the
South after his heart's desire.

Once, on the Day of Atonement, when R. Paltiel was called   18c
to read from the Torah, the whole assemblage arose and remained
standing in his presence, the sages, the scholars that were in the
school,[1] the young students and the elders, the lads and children;
the entire community was standing.   He called to them saying,
"Let the old be seated, and the young stand.   If you refuse, I
will sit down and refuse to read, for this does not seem right to
me."   When he finished reading, he vowed to the God of his
praise 5000 dinars[2] of genuine and full value; 1000 for the head
of the academy and the sages, 1000 for the mourners of the
sanctuary, 1000 for the academy of Geonim at Babylon, 1000
for the poor and needy of the various communities, and 1000
for the exaltation of the Torah, for the purchase of the necessary
oil.   In the morning he arose early and hurried, for he was always
zealous in observing the law, that his evil inclination might not
prevail over him to prevent his carrying out his good intention;
he engaged men and horses and mules, and provided guards, and
sent them forth with the caravans that travelled through the

[1] Abrahams, *Jewish Life in Middle Ages, 317.*
[2] Above, *65, n. 2.*

deserts. And they delivered the gold pieces, as R. Paltiel their master had ordered, and distributed them among the schools and synagogs, and the mourners of Zion and the poor of the communities of Israel.[1]

The growth of his authority which the king, through his bounty, had bestowed upon him over his royal domain, having appointed him ruler over the kingdom of Egypt and of Syria as far as Mesopotamia, and over all (that had once been) the land of Israel as far as Jerusalem, his eminence and power and wealth[2] with which the king had honored and distinguished him, are recorded in the chronicles of the kingdom of Nof[3] and Anamim (Egypt). 19a

When Al Muizz was stricken with the sickness of which he was to die, he placed his son[4] on the throne and entrusted him to R. Paltiel, his beloved minister, that he might be his adviser and helper and guardian, that he might govern the kingdom with vigor and success. The Caliph died and slept with his fathers and his son reigned in his stead. All his days had been passed in happiness and security, in peace and content. 19b

When (the young caliph) sat upon the throne of his kingdom, the officials appointed to conduct the affairs of Egypt told him lying stories about R. Paltiel, continually striking at him with the sharp sword of their tongues, and covertly slandering him.[5] The Caliph's fury raged against them; he repeatedly rebuked them. He told R. Paltiel, the prince, all they said. So together they devised a plan of dealing with them. R. Paltiel and his wife, and friends and all his family went out to his estate, the royal garden that the Caliph had presented to him. 19c

In words of affection the Caliph asked, "Whither has our beloved R. Paltiel, the interpreter of mysteries, gone?" The attendants assembled in the court answered "He has gone out for recreation, with his friends and all his kin, to the estate[6] which 19d

---

[1] Here and elsewhere the Chronicle dwells upon the chief objects of consideration and benevolence. Below *97*.

[2] In Hebrew Text 19 l. 7 read וְעָשְׁרוֹ.

[3] Ezekiel 30, 13, 16; I Chronicles 1, 11; Kaufmann, *536*.

[4] Above, *27*.

[5] Above, *27*.

[6] I. e., garden-palace.

the king has given him." Thereupon the king summoned his magistrates, princes and courtiers, and said to them, "We will go and pay our respects to the venerable scholar in my service, R. Paltiel, so highly esteemed and worthy of honor at my hands." He set out in his chariot and took with him all his lords and princes. The king did this with set purpose; all of this being done as a ruse, ordered by the word of the king, that he might find opportunity to show R. Paltiel his intense love for him, in the presence of the courtiers and princes of the people, to confound his accusers, and cover them with shame and confusion. And as the king drew near the tent of R. Paltiel, he commanded that no one should inform him until he reached the tent. The king descended from the chariot and R. Paltiel approached him. The king, out of his love for him, embraced, caressed and kissed him, and took hold of his hands. They walked away together and took their seats apart from the company. The others remained where they were. Then the jesters and players appeared; they took up the harps and timbrels and made merry before them with the pipes, with stringed instruments and songs, playing upon timbrels, cymbals and harps, from morning until the decline of the day in the afternoon, until evening when the shadow begins to move backward. The king then rode off and returned to Egypt (i.e., to the city). So the face of the accusers was covered with confusion, the enemies and slanderers of R. Paltiel were put to shame. On that day their tongues were silenced, and they did not again speak ill of him. Praised be He that protecteth His saints, that redeemeth and saveth the soul of His servants. Praised be He and praised be His name; praised be the glory of God from His place.

One night R. Paltiel and the king were walking in the open 20a and they saw three bright stars disappear; in an instant their light had vanished. And R. Paltiel said, "The stars that have been eclipsed represent three kings who will die this year; and they will soon be taken off. The first king is John[1] the Greek, the second, the king of Bagdad, in the north"; then the king

---

[1] Kaufmann, *537 n. 2; ZDMG 51, 441 n. 2.*

hastening to interrupt him said, "Thou art the third, the King of Teman,"[1] but he replied to the king, "No, my Lord, for I am a Jew; the third is the king of Spain." But the king said, "Thou art in truth the third, as I say."

And in that year R. Paltiel died, the leader of the community 20b of the people of God, settled in Egypt and Palestine, in Palermo[2] and in Africa, and in all the territory of the Arabians (Ishmael), for he ruled over the (ancient) kingdom of the Hebrews, over that of the Syrians and Egyptians, over the domain of the Arabians and the land of Israel. May his soul be bound in the bundle of life, secure in Eden, enclosed in the Garden of God, reposing by the side of the Fathers.

In his stead arose his son R. Samuel, a great man, highly 20c esteemed in his day, (worthily) filling the place of his father. He brought the remains of his father and mother in caskets to Jerusalem, also the casket containing the bones of R. Hananeel, his father's uncle, which had been embalmed. He devoted[3] to the Most High, that it might be counted as righteousness unto him, by Him that rideth upon the clouds, 20000 drachmae for the poor and afflicted, for the sages and teachers giving instruction in the law, for the instructors of the children and the readers (of prayer); and for the oil of the sanctuary, at the western wall of the inner altar, and for the synagogs and communities, far and near; for those who mourned the loss of the Temple, those who grieved and sorrowed for Zion;[4] for the academy of the disciples and the teachers (in Palestine), and for the sages of Babylon in the academy of the Geonim. Blessed be his memory. May his life be prolonged, partaking of the feast of the living, sustained through the treasures of God.

I[5] will ascribe righteousness unto my God; I will praise 20d and magnify my Creator. I will exalt, in words of song, the Lord, God of my veneration (prayer). In the assembly of the

---

[1] Jeremiah 49, 7; Kaufman, *ZDMG 51, 438 n. 2.*

[2] The name of the capital city probably implies Sicily as a whole.

[3] Above, *95 n. 1.*

[4] Krauss, *Studien;* Bacher, *REJ 32, 149 n. 1.*

[5] The double alphabetical acrostic beginning here is best explained as an elegy in memory of Paltiel.

congregation I will utter praise to His name, in fear and trembling entreating Him that worketh wonders, acknowledging the greatness of His glory; proclaiming the eternal sway of His power, with tuneful words of prayer I will call upon Him. Telling of His glorious deeds, I will at all times speak of His dominion, treading His paths in uprightness, proclaim Him to coming generations. Eagerly, fervidly will I delight in prayer and song. The majesty of my God in heaven, I will ever declare. The might of His signs and wonders He hath shown in all lands; He will reward His afflicted children for their radiant good deeds. He visited His mercy and kindness upon the descendants of His two beloved servants; He extended over the house of His servants the reward of the merit and righteousness of His pious ones; He saved them from (the oppressor's) fury and violence, and delivered them from trouble and distress; with boundless love for them, He delivered them from the affliction of cruel laws; He adorned them with that which is more precious than pearls, sweeter than honey to the palate. He (exalted) in purity, whose eyes are upon the faithful, upheld them and provided them with food.

They had lived in Oria, in prosperity, for seventeen Jubilee (periods), when the king of the Arabians fell upon them,[1] expelled them from the land. Madly and violently he overran and devastated Calabria; he subdued the country from the harbor and extended his conquest into the province of Longobardia; he made havoc in the land, and reduced it to the extremity of distress; he took them captive to his country to let their souls languish in utter desolation. But the Exalted One in heaven, that looketh upon the depths and causeth them to tremble, that commandeth and controlleth all the powers (foundations) of the universe, let the children of His upright servants find mercy before Him; from above, the merit of the ancient fathers was remembered for their sake. The king looked about carefully and wisely saw among them the sage, a master of astrology and secret wisdom. He elevated him over all his counselors and gave him charge of his treasures. In his time the Jews prospered as the Jordan in the

---

[1] Kaufmann, *553 note 2.*

overflow of its waters. He was appointed vizier and prince,[1] second in authority in the palace of the king, making happy use of his possessions; refuting the unbelievers and heretics. He prospered and shone in his greatness, his giving became more extended, his offerings and gifts increased, to those who loved God and His law; he devoted and distributed money to the poor of Jerusalem and the cities (of the Dispersion); he remembered the established schools, the sages and scholars; uprightness issued from his loins. With a master's grasp of the Law, he defeated the traitor and heretic, and helped and saved the innocent. Alert to do good, serving God in love, he kept His commandments with ardent and happy devotion; an upright man, consecrating gifts to Him whose majesty and power reach to the heavens; patron of the disciples of the schools; giving strength to the broken-hearted, through intense, sincere affection.

The awe-inspiring God bestowed upon them knowledge, understanding and judgment, (sound) wisdom and power; He that putteth on light (as a garment) adorned them with insight and learning, with abundance of wealth and honor. The God of light blessed them with the spirit of reverence and whole-souled humility; the Creator of the world heartened them with (His) ordinances, and led them in the way of wisdom whose gain is better than silver, more precious than pearls. He that answereth the remnant of His upright ones in time of trial girded them with strength, gave them dominion and authority; by the power of His spirit He sustained the resplendent heavens for their descendants and led them safely; He was their shield and place of refuge; a high wall and fenced city; a tower of strength to their children, a help and place of shelter. He gave them the rewards of victory and He enlarged their boundaries; He prospered the work of their hands; He bestowed His blessing upon their treasures, and granted peace and security to their homes, content and happiness with their possessions.

[1] This reference to Paltiel as Nagid, the earliest that we have to this highest dignity among the Jews of Egypt, may well mean that it was first bestowed by Al Muizz upon his favorite vizier. Kaufmann, 535 note 1; Mann *I*, *252*.

When their descendants came to Capua, God let them win 21a
the favor of their rulers; the rulers of the city took R. Samuel
to their palace and appointed him supervisor of their treasury,
that he should have jurisdiction in their realm, over the ports
of the harbor, over the income of their markets, and over the
finances of the various departments of the city. And the God
of our fathers helped him. And he visited R. Paltiel at times
to exchange greetings, and remained several days each time.
God granted him rest on every hand and made him happy with
the knowledge of the law of delight and enriched him with property. He was engaged with all his means in having Torah scrolls
written and he erected houses of prayer. God gave him a
worthy son, whom he named Paltiel, walking in the ways of God,
devoted to the law of Israel. He did not stray from the ways of
his father, and was steadfast in the fear of God, in wisdom and
understanding; his home did not lack any of the blessings of God.
The prince appointed him governor and director of all the affairs
of the city; over prince, noble, counsellor, judges, officials, and
all administrators, over all of them he was chief magistrate. His
was the authority to receive and dismiss, to direct and command.
But he held fast to the statutes of God and His Law, and loved
His commandments and ordinances, serving Him with all his
heart; declaring His unity with all his soul. He restored the
synagog of his grandfather as a house of prayer, for the glory
of Him that dwelleth above. He had no children; for those that
had been born to him had died when they were but two or three
years of age. In his anguish and affliction, he prayed in fervent
supplication to Him that inhabiteth the heavens. And God
from the heavens of His splendor heard his prayer and cry, and
in His mercy and kindness gave him an only son. He named
him Ahimaaz. He sent him to school to be instructed in the
Law, to give thought to the Scriptures, the unfailing testimony,
to their wholesome teaching, their sublime commandments, to
(learn to) observe their precepts. 22a

And I, Ahimaaz, son of R. Paltiel, son of R. Samuel, son of
R. Hananeel, son of R. Amittai, the servant of God; in the
first month of the year 4814 since the heavens were made, asked

a boon of Him, that He might enlighten me in the mysteries of the everlasting delight, that He might confirm me in His perfect Law, handed down thousands of years ago; that He might lead me in the right path and help me; that He might hearken to my prayer, to let me succeed in finding the genealogy of my fathers. I looked to Him and trusted in His holy name and besought His grace and mercy. He has granted the wish I have so ardently asked of Him. I have pondered and examined and have found what my heart desired, the lineage of my family. With God's help I have arranged and written it in poetic form. I have begun at the very beginning; from the captivity of Jerusalem and the destruction of the house of our (my) glory, through the captivity of the city of Oria, in which I have settled, I have come down to the arrival of my fathers in Capua; and have ended with my own time and that of my children. In a book I have collected and compiled and narrated it for the generations to come. I have clearly unfolded and explained it. I give praise to my God, and glorify His majesty and power, and in His glorious presence I offer honor and thanks that He has helped me complete the book I have planned. In the month of Sivan I have finished it; under the sign of the Twins,[1] under which our Torah was given, in the year 4814, in accordance with my desire, I have completed it from beginning to end. Praised be the radiance of His Shechina's glory and the splendor of His divine throne; exalted be His name, and the name of the glory of His Kingdom.

I will attempt to determine the number of years from the days 22b of R. Shephatiah and R. Hananeel to the time of R. Ahimaaz, son of R. Paltiel. The persecution decreed by Basil the wicked tyrant occurred in the year 4628. R. Shephatiah and R. Hananeel lived at that time. After R. Hananeel's death there was his son R. Hasadiah; R. Hasadiah begat R. Paltiel; R. Paltiel begat Hananeel. And in the year 4700 there arose, with the help of the Lord of wonders, R. Samuel his son, who ended his devotion to the Lord of Hosts when he was 68 years old. And in the year 4748, R. Paltiel, his son, was born; in 803 his

---

[1] Above, *62 n. 7.*

soul returned to his Master. In 777 his son R. Ahimaaz was born. May He, enthroned among the Cherubim, be his help and support and prolong his years, for the sake of His throne of glory. In 798,[1] his son,[2] R. Paltiel, was born, and in 804 God blessed him with a second son whom he named R. Samuel. May the Lord God of Israel, grant them long life. In their day, may the altar[3] be rebuilt and the sanctuary, called the hearth of God; and the redeemer appear, Menahem ben Amiel,[4] Nehemiah ben Hoshiel, to gather and redeem the scattered children of the house of Jacob, shortly and in our day, in the day of the whole house of Israel. Amen.

In the year 4814 of the creation of the world which God has   23a created, I compiled this book of my genealogy with the help of God, my refuge, not by any wisdom that is in me, or intelligence of my own, but by the grace of the Lord God my master.

Praised be He that giveth power to the faint and deliverance to him that hath no might.[5]

Completed by Menahem son of Benjamin. May the Creator of the left and the right, be their help.

[1] This date of Paltiel's birth, 4728, would more correctly be 4798, as suggested by Kaufmann.

[2] Zunz, *SP 427*.

[3] Ezekiel 43, 15, *16*.

[4] A fervid expression of the belief, common in the author's day and dating from the third century, in the Messiah, son of Joseph, appointed to assemble and redeem the outcasts of Israel, to make ready for the final salvation under the Messiah, Son of David. A conspicuous figure in rabbinical apocalyptic literature, he is known by these names, symbolical of Divine comfort and redemption. Buttenwieser, *Messiah, JE VIII. 511 b;* Greenstone, *The Messiah Idea in Jewish History, 135;* Hamburger, *REII, 768.*

[5] Isaiah, 61, 2; 40, 29.

INDEX

ספר יוהסין

חברו

הרב אחימאץ בן פלטיאל

ספר יוחסין

ספר יוחסין

בשם אדוני האדונ[ים   ¹] עושה נסים לכתוב ספר .... ² יוחסין:

בשם שוכן שמי שפר אתחיל להליץ ולספר לחקור ולדרוש ולחפר תקון מדרש
ספר ספר האיגרונים מאבות הראשונים להביע בעניונים לפרש בהגיונים אגור
בקש ³ היחם לבקש בלי להנקש מבקש ומראש ומתחילה אתן תהילה ושבח וגדולה
לרב העלילה שם קדשו אהללה נצח זכרו אגדלה שבחו אסלסלה במורה ובחילה
כמאז ומקדם תפארתו אקיצה ולא אהיה רודם בדברי פי לקדם ⁴ מעונה אלהי
קדם אהל בשיח ומענים להפגיע תחנונים באמת ובאמונים פני שוכן מעונים לשנן
בשיונים לנגן בניגונים לעלם ברנים לאדוני האדונים במושב זקנים בחבורת
נבונים לשבח בעיצומים לחי העולמים לפאר באיומים לרם על כל רמים להכתיר
בהילומים ליושב מרומים בקיבוץ תמימים בועד חכמים וימים ולילות אנעים
תהלות לעושה גדולות למרעים בקולות לאלהים צבאות המפליא פלאות ועשה
גדולות ⁵ לראות קדומי להראות נסים ונפלאות לטובה אות אהלל ברננה לדר
מעונה לנגן בנגינה בשפך תחינה ביראה ובינה באימה ובנ[חלח]לה ¹ נכונה בעמק
שושנה להגיד גבורותיו ל[ספר] ¹ נפלאותיו ותוקף גדולותיו ויקר תושבחותיו ואומץ
גבורותיו ונועם תהילותיו ועוצם נוראותיו וחוזק ממשלותיו שהפליא בניצוחו לגדיל
שבחו המכין הרים בכוחו ומגיד לאדם מה שיחו עושה ארץ בחכמתו מכין תבל
בתבונותו ומי יערוך לו בשחקים וממשלתו בכל קצוי ארקים והים מנים בגערתו
ודרי חלד יתבהלון מאימתו ההרים ירקדון משאיתו והגבעות תמוטנה בהבטתו
ויגדל כחו וגבורתו בכל מקומות ממשלתו ויתעלה ויתנשא זיו הדרתו ויתברך
שמו ושם כבוד מלכותו:

אפאר בהילולים לדר בזבולים אשר בטוב מפעלים ובכושר מעללים נוהג
ביושר שבילים אבותי המוגלים הבאים עם הגולים אשר בירושלים נצלים והציל
מביהולים צעירים וגדולים שבים ועוללים למען רחמיו העצומים וזכות אבות
הקדומים ומאת שוכן מעונים בכל עת ממונגים וצינה ומנינים מאז ומלפנים היה
בכל זמנים לאבותי הקדמונים ויהיה בכל עדנים לבנים ולבני בנים ולבני בניהם
האח[רונים] ¹ ובכן אערוכה לסדר כהלכה בשקט ושככה [   ] ¹ לערכה מאבותי
כהובאו באנייה בנהר פ[שון] ¹ נהר עדן ראשון עם הגולה אשר טיטוס הנ[לה מן] ¹

---

* Abbreviation for יי   .בעזרת יי נתחיל ונגמור עזרי מעם יי   ¹ Injured.
² So MS.   ³ MS. בקש.   ⁴ B. for MS. לקיים.   ⁵ Injured ; K., נוראות.

3

העיר ביופי כלולה ובאורי¹ עלו ושם נקהלו [ו]נדלו² ובמעשים נתעלו ורבו ופרו
ועצמו וגב[רו]² עמד מהם מניניהם מבני בניהם איש חכם בתור[ה]² פייט
וסבר בדת אל גבר נבון בעמו ור´ אמתי שמו ולו היו⁸ בנים נאים והגונים
חכמים ונבונים דעתנים ופייטנים מלמדים ומשננים לתלמידים המהוגנים נסיכים
נגדים מביני סודים חרוזי חרזים יודעי רזים בחכמה צופים בבינה מצפים ובערמה
מצפצפים בספר הישר משכילים ובסוד המרכבה מסתכלים הראשון ר´ שפטיה
העוסק בתושיה והשני ר´ חנגאל ההוגה בדת אל שהוריד יקותיאל ואלעזר השלישי
הצופה בניתנה בשלישי ובימי אלה החסידים ירד מן הידידים איש חמודים מארץ
בגדידים⁴ ראש ואב מבית יואב ושמו אהרן סבר בסברון עוצר חרן מניני⁵
ישיני חברון והוא כבני מרון למלך אדירידרון:

טרם צאתו מארץ מולדתו לאביו היה ריחים למחיה והפרד שהיה גוללו בא
הארי ואכלו ואהרן היה חוצה כשחזר למחיצה הפרד לא מצא ותחת פרדו הביא
הארי וניגדו וכפתו בריחים לטחון⁶ בעדו ואביו כשהרגיש אליו הגיש וזעק לו
וצעק בקולו ודיבר למולו מה עשית הארי הבאת ולהכניעו כוחו שיברת והקבה
עשהו מלך [בקו]מה⁷ זקופה לילך ואתה שמתו בעבודתך לעשות שיר[ותך]⁷ ועתה
חי אדני אם תעמד לפניי ותצא בגלות [יומם]² ולילות ועד שלש שנים תתנחם
על שנייונים [ואחר]² שוב לארצך ויי אלהיך ירצך:

בא עד יפו [ואניות]² מצא מפה ומפה אמר למלחים רעים ואהובים [בשם
שוכן הכרובים אכנס]⁸ ביניכם ואבוא עמכם וארשה בגזירה ברשות דר נהורה
שהספפינה שאנו בה יושבים אינה חושמת מאויבים ולא מרוח סערה בעזרת אל
נורא נכנס ביניהם וישב עמהם ובשעת הלינה והם בגאיטה המדינה מצא שם
ביחידי איש אחד יהודי והוא היה ספרדי הוליכו עמו וכיבדו בעצמו⁹ בא עת
האוכל והספרדי לא היה אוכל ואותו היום היה שבת הקודש ליה הרב שאלו
להבין מילולו שבת היום לנורא ואיום ולמה לא תתענג בקראוי עונג ענה העני
ואמר אי אדוני אל תעניישיני כי מר נפשי אני ומתאבל על בני שנכסה ממני
מרוב עווני ואיני יודע באמת אם חי הוא אם מת השיב לו בחיבת תן כבוד
לשבת והראיני ארחות ומעגלות שהיה רגיל לירד ולעלות אם בחיים עודהו אצלך
אביאהו ואם גזור הוא מארץ אגיד לך בחריץ ליום מחר לא איחר והלכו ביחד¹⁰
בדרך אחד אל בית ריעיהם שבנו נהוג ללכת אליהם ושם אשה דרה כשפנית
היתה הארורה ובכשפיה בשפה והנער לחמור חילפה¹¹ ובריחים העמידו לטחן
כל ימי עודו החכם כראהו בן והכיר מראהו ולאביו הקשב הנה בנך מישב אשר

¹ K. for N. ובאורן.   ² MS. injured.   ³ MS. היה.   ⁴ MS. בגדידים.
⁵ K. and B. for N. מניני.   ⁶ K. for N. לטען.   ⁷ MS. end of line שׁיר,
beginning of next injured.   ⁸ MS. injured; reading suggested by K.
⁹ K. for N. בעצמו.   ¹⁰ MS. ביחד.   ¹¹ K. and B. for N. חולפה.

כמה נחשב אליך קרא לאשת[1] ואמר לה בארשת למה לא תכלמי בבושת מאשר
לכדת ברשת והשיבי להורו בנו ובשרו והזונה נשכחה לדבר[י]ו לא[2] השגיחה
ודבר לא השיבה לא באהבה ולא באיבה הצדיק מה עשה החמור תפש בתפישה
וחוצה הוציא אותו וחילף דמותו ומראיתו והשיבו לצורתו כשהיה בק[דמתו][3]
ולאביו החזירו ונתן שבח ליוצרו ושבחו ליוצרם אשר בראם :

ואחרי זאת הבין לחזות לעשות עזיזות קשות ועזות בביניבינטו בלכתו יצאו
[לק]ראתו[2] כל הקהל ביחד כולם כאיש אחד וביום השבת עמד בחור אחד נחמד
לעשות תפילה לפני שוכן מעלה והתפילה הנעים בקול נעים ובהגיע בברכו את יי
המבורך קולו בנעם ארך והשם לא הזכיר והרב הבין והכיר שהמתפלל מת היה
ולא המתים יהללויה מיד זעק ובקול גדול צעק שב אל תתהלל שאינך ראוי להלל
ולפני אל להתפלל התחיל לפייסו ולהשביעו בעושו הגד לי ואל תפחד ומעשיך
מני אל תכחד והודה האמת האמת ליוצר[4] הרוח נוצר ושים נא כבוד לאל הכבוד ותן
לו תודה בתוך קהל ועדה וקנה העולם הבא ובזה אל יהי לך חובה ותינצל מחובה
ותקנה לעצמך טובה והעולם הארוך והטוב הערוך לצדיקי עמו ליראי יי ולחושבי
שמו מיד ענה ואמר אמנה אנכי חטאתי ולי[4] עויתי ומרדתי ופשעתי והרע עשיתי
ואם תקבלו הפשע שעבדכם פשע והם קיבלו כולהם כל אשר שם עליהם ואז
הודה ולאלהים נתן תודה והגיד שעשה וכל אשר בו נעשה שמעני עם יי אלופי
רבני ישישיי וזקיניי חכמיי נבוני קציניי ורומניי גדולי וקטניי אגיד לכם בפירוש
כל המעשה לפרש :

איש יהודי היה ביומו ור אחימעץ שמו בירושלים עיר ההוללה[1] פעמים שלש
בנדרים עלה ובכל פעם עלייתו מאה זהובים הוליך אתו שכן היתה נדרבתו פני
צור ישועתו להטיב לעוסקי בתורתו ולאבילי זבול תפארתו ובפעם השלישי שעלה
לאמי שאלני בשאילה תניהו לי להיות אצלי לעלות עמי להנאת עצמי ולעשות
שירותי ואני אוליכנו מידי תבקשנו ואם לא אביאנו וחטאתי לי[4] אני ובניי אז
הלב[נ]ו[5] בשמחה בלי יגון ואנחה כשהיינו יושבים בסעודה מסובים עם ראש
הישיבה ותלמידי הרחבה פצחו בפציחה נתן שבחה וזמרה חביבה ושירה עריבה
באהב ובחיבה לרגול מרבבה נתנו עיניהם בתלמידיהם היושבים לפניהם וראש
הישיבה שלהם הביט אליהם ואמר להם הבחור היושב ביניני שבא עם ר אחימעץ
חבירינו הוא ישמחינו וייטב לבינו[5] בפוץ מעייניו בשיח הגיוניו התחלתי[6] בשירה
בניגון וזמרה להלל במורה לעוטה אורה :

ושם ישב זקן ושב ושריי קשב ובליבו חשב התחיל לבכות ועיניו שופכות
במר בכות ור אחימעץ בט אליו והבין מעלליו וקם מן המסיבה ולפני רגליו בא
ובאלהים[7] השביעו בכייתו להודיעו ועונה באמירה וידעו בברירה שיצאה גזירה

---

[1] So MS.   [2] Injured.   [3] Injured; מ visible.   [4] So margin;
text לאל = לא.   [5] MS. וייטב ליבינו.   [6] MS. ה. התחלתי.   [7] MS.
והאלהים.

מלפני הגבורה בודאי ובאמת שהנער הזה מהרה הוא מת הוא החסיר כשמע
ועיניו דמעו דמע בגדיו קרע וראשו פרע והשיב לכולם אין לי חיים בעולם
שעשיתי לאמו שבועה להשיבו אליה בלי אסון ורעה ואיך אשוב לביתי והנער
איננו אתי והשבועה שנשבעתי יאבד תקוותי וסבר תוחלתי כשראו בצרתו ואבל
בכייתו כתבו שם הנקדש שהיה כתוב במקדש ובבשר חתכוני בזרוע ימיני ובמקום
שהבשר חתכו שמה השם ערכו ומשם בשלום באתי ולביתי ולאמי שבתי ועד
שהיה ר' אחימעץ בחיים ברחתי מאיים לאיים ועתה אני חי מאותם הימים אם
אני רוצה לעולמים כי מקום השם אין אדם יודע רק אם אני אודיע אבל אני
מראה לכם והנני בידכם עשו לי כטוב בעיניכם והביאו השמלה ועליה עלה
והראה מקום הקרע והרב שם קרע ומתוכו הוציא השם והגוף נשאר בלא נשם
ונפל הגולם רקב כמשנים רבות נרקב והבשר שבה לעפרה [ולרקבונה והנפש
הלכה לאלהים אשר נתנה] : [1]

ומשם נסע ואל אורי [2] פסע ומצא שם אהלים נטועים בנחלים וכעצים שתולים
עלי מים גדילים ומדרשות קבועים כארזים נטועים בעל מים שוכנים ביבלי מעינים
ולוחמים ומתגברים במלחמת שערים ודורשים ברבים באילת אהבים ובעלת חינים
הם נושאים ונותנים הם הם הרשומים אחים הנעימים בני ר' אמיתי הם אבות
אבותי ר' שפטיה ור' חננאל שניהם עבדי אל מעצימים הלל לאלהי ישראל ותחן
שופכים ושבח עורכים וקדושה מנסכים ומעריצים וממליכים כערך המלאכים
למלך מלכי המלכים וביניהם נקבע וישבתו שם קבע והכמתו נבעה ותורתו שם
נטעה ושם הראה אונים והפסקת דיינים כבהיות האורים וישיבת סנהדרין ותורת
הסוטה ושם איהל והיטה ותחת עפר קרקע המשכן עפר יסוד ארון הוכן [3] ואחד [4]
תופילו מעל מעילה ובא על אשה בעולה ודנו בווער בין קהילה בחנק היות לכלה
ואיש אחד [5] קפץ לרגלה על אשה אחת והרנה ופסק דינו לתונה וצוה עליו [6]
הרינה ואחר בא אל הזכר עשה כעובדי אל נכר ודינו נודע והוכר ולסקילה נכאב
ונעכר [7] אחד בא אל חמותו עבר על דת אל ותורתו וצוה הרב בצואתו נוערו
אליו ושרפו אותו :

וברחמי בכוחו ארץ עושה עובר על פשע עון ונושא אמליץ ואזכיר המעשה
אשר אירע בבינוסי איש בא מארץ ישראל מבין ויודע בתורת אל ומשכיל
באמון שעשועים ושהה שם ימים ושבועים והיה עושה בכל שבת דרשה בתוך
הכנסת בעם ‏ה‏ לדרשה והחכם היה דורש ור' סילנו היה מפרש ויום אחד באו
האנשים בעגנות מן הכפרים אל המדינה לעלות ועשו מריבה האנשים ביניהם
ותצאנה הנשים מבתיהן [8] ובעצים הארוכים אשר התנור מחככים ומן האש

---

[1] Added by K.; no indication of injury or omission in MS.
[2] K. for N. אורן.   [3] B. for text היכן.   [4] MS. ואחת.   [5] MS. אחת.
[6] MS. עליה.   [7] K. and N. for text ובנכר.   [8] K., for האנשים מבתיהם.

מחורכים בהם היו האנשים והנשים מכים ור' סילנו שגג וטעה בליבו חשב ועשה
רעה הביא המדרש מן הפרשה שבאותה שבת החכם עתיד לפרשה ומחק שתי
שורות מן האותיות אשר שם היו חרותות ובאותו המקום כתב המעשה אשר
למעלה נכתב וזה כתב הנחרת שר' סילנו חרת באו האנשים בקרון ותצאנה [1]
הנשים מפורנן והכו האנשים בפורקן וביום השבת בהגיע החכם באותם המילים
החסים לשונו ומילתו האלים והביט האותיות והבין וסבר ועליהם פעם ופעמיים
עבר ולפי תומו קרא והדברים שמצא כתובים הורה ור' סילנו בלצון וצחק לכל
היושבים השיב בשחק שמעו שהרב דורש לכם המריבה שאתמול נעשתה ביניכם
כשהכו הנשים את האנשים והכום בעצי התנורים והבריחום מכל עברים החכם
כראה והבין נתכרכמו פניו והלבין ועלה אל החבירים אשר בישיבה סבורים
וסיפר להם הפנע רע אשר אליו הוגע [2] ואירע ונתעצבו כולם בעצבון ודאגו בינן
ובדאבון ובירכו ר' סילנו הנבון :

ועמד בנידויו ימים ושנים מאוחרים עד עלות שם ר' אחימעץ עם הנדרים
והתיר להם הנדוי בחכמתו שמעו מה שעשה בתבונתו בשעלה היו עשרת ימי
תשובה ופייסוהו החבירים וראש הישיבה לעמוד לפני התיבה ולעשות התפילה
בחיבה לפני אל נערץ בסוד קדושים רבה וכן עשה בעינוותנותו ושהיה בליבו
יראת שמים ואימתו התחיל בסליחות ותחנונים ערב ריינונים [3] באחד שהיה ר'
סילנו איש אמונים שהתחלתו אלה [4] וכחש ורצח וכחש וכנע בזכר קדמונים
החליף רבנים וגרמו חמנים חילף המינים כשהשלים התפילה שאלוהו בשאילה מי
היה פה המחבב שהחכמים כל כך חיבב ומי היה פה הקדושה שכך עשה תפילה
בקרושה שאהב ועילה הרבנים וריחק ותיעב המינים השיב להם בתשובה הוא ר'
סילנו הפה החביבה אשר ביניכם אשר לתועבה מיד עמדו כולם על רגליהם
והתירו החרם והנידוי אשר שמו לו בפיהם ושמו לו ברכה גדולה וארוכה סדורה
וערוכה וענו ביחד כולם מבורך ר' סילנו לעולם :

ובאותו הזמן ובאותם הימים מלך מלך על אדומים איש עוולה ומרמה בדמים
חשב בלבו וזמם להחרים יחוד הצור פעולו פעולי תמים מפי זרע קדושים ותמימים
בשנת שמנה מאות שנים לעיר הקודש למלאות חרבנים לגלות יהודים וישראלים
לחורבן המקרש בית זבולים קם עובד חמן [5] להשחית עם לא אלמן מלך ושמו
בסילי עמד לעקם שבילי למחות שם ושארית פליטת ישראל להכרית להמות[ם] [6]
מתורה ולהטעותם ברת יאושה וצוה במרוצות [7] בכל ארצות ורוכבי סוסים שלח
בכל אפסים בממשלת ידו היושבים נגדו להשיב היהודים מאמונתם ואחר [8] ההבל
להטעותם והשלוחים שטטו עד המעבר באורדרנטו ושם נכנסו [9] באניה ועברו

---

[1] MS. ויצאו האנשים.   [2] K., הגיע.   [3] B. for N. עד בריגונים (MS. ער).
[4] Quotation from a poem of R. Silano.   [5] MS. חמן.   [6] Injured.
[7] K. for N. במריצות.   [8] On margin by later hand; erased in original.
[9] K. for MS. נכנס.

באָרץ פולייה ובהגיע השמועה והארץ התרועעה וסבבו הארץ מפינה לפינה ובאו
עד אויירי המדינה והביאו כתב עם חותם בחותמת המלך מחותם והחותם כרוסבולי
מזהב היה ששלח המלך לו שפטיה :

ואלה דברי האגרת אשר שם היו חרותים בחרת אני בסילי המלך שלחתי
אליך ר' שפטיה להביאך בהלך ואתה אלי תבוא ולא תמנע מבוא כי שמעתי
חכמתך ורוב בינתך והרב תורתך ותאוותי לראותך ונשבעתי בנפשי ובכתר
ראשי כי שלום יהיה ביאתך וכמוכן¹ אחזירך לביתך וכבוד לך אעשה כמו
לקרובי הייתי עושה ובקשה אחת שתשאל ממני בשאילה אמלא חפצך באהבה
גדולה :

אז נכנס אל הספינה ועלה לקוסטנטינא אשר קוסטנטינו המלך בנה האלהים
ישבר נאונה ועמה וכל המונה ו-ה' אלהים נתנו לפני המלך ובחינו ומצא חן בעיניו
ובעין כל המונו :

אז נכנס עמו בדברי תורה ושאלו מבניין בית הבחירה ומבניין הטומאה אשר
סופיאה קרואה באי זה ארמון נכנס יותר ממון המלך היה מקשה ובבנין סופיאה
היה מתקשה כי זה הבנין נכנס שם בלא קנין והוא השיבו בדיברה מילה נכונה
וסדורה אם מלפני אדוני גזירה יביאו לפניו המקרא ושם תמצא העיקר אי זה
בניין היה יקר מיד עשה כן ומצא את התוכן כל התוכן אשר דוד ושלמה תיכן יותר על
המדה אשר בסופיאה נמדרה מזהב ככרים מאה ועשרים ומן הכסף ככרים חמש
מאות בתוסף אז אמר המלך באמרתו נצחני ר' שפטיה בחכמתו והוא ענה ואמר
אדוני נצחתך המקרא ולא אני :

ואחרי כן זמנו לאכל על שלחנו לפניו להברות מגדים ופירות ומזהב קערות
לפניו היו סדורות לאכול בטהרה כציווי התורה ובשלשלות שלכסף חמורות היו
הקערות יורדות וממקום שהקערות יורדות לפניו לא היה איש רואה בעיניו :

ולבסילי הי[ת]ה בת שהיה מחבבה כבבת והשד היה מצער אותה ולא היה
יכול לרפאותה וקראו בסתר וחינן לו בעתר עזרני שפטיה ורפא בתי מחולייה
השיב לו כן אעשה בוודאי בעזרת אל שדי שאלו יש לך מקום סגול שלא יהיה
שם מקום פגול ענה המלך בקליאן² מהוגן ויש לי הגן ראה הוא והוא וישר
בקליאן² בעיניהו שפתרונו פי ארי בעיניונהו והביא שם העלמה והשביע השד
בשם שוכן רומה ובשם פועל רום והרומה ובשם יסד ארץ בחכמה ובשם יוצר
הרים וימה ובשם תולה ארץ על בלימה והשד היה צוח על מה אתה מרוח לבת
הרשע שנגבר ברשע והרבה להרשע על עם נשע ומי- לי היא מסורה³ להכניעה
ולשברה ועתה לך מעמי כי לא אצא ממקומי והוא אל השד השיב לדבריך אינני
מקשיב צא בשם אל שם אל וידע כי יש אלהים בישראל מיד יצא וברח במרוצה והוא

תפשו ובכלי שלאבר הכניסו והכלי מפו ומפו כיסו וחותמו בשם עושו ואל הים
טיבעו ובתוך מים אדירים שקעו והנערה הלכה בשקט ושכבה בשלום אל המלך
ואל המלכה :

ואז בא אל המלך לקבל רשותו והמלך יצא לקראתו ונתן זרועו בצואריו
והוליכו אל חדריו והתחיל לפתותו מן האמונה לנסותו ברוב מתנתו *אחר ההבל
להטעותו[1] וחוצה יצא עמו ופיו קרא להולמו ובא אליו במכמן ורעים עליו זימן[2]
כשראה[3] הארון הכעס והזדון צוח בקול גדול להכביר אדוני אביר ביה את עלי
מעביר בכן עמד המלך מכסאו ומתוך העם נשאו ונתן לו רשות לילכה ושילחו
אל המלכה ליתן לו מתנה וברכה והמלכה שאלו בעיינים[4] יש לך בנות ובנים
והוא השיבה[5] תשובות מוכנות יש לעבדך בן אחד ושתי בנות ונתנה לו הנזמים
שבאזניה והאזור אשר במתניה והשביעו למען תורתך תן אותם לשתי בנותיך כי
בשווה דמיהם וערך אין להם וליטרא זהב היה היה משקל הנזמים והאזור כן היה
שווה בדמים :

ומאחר שנטל לילך בפיו קראו המלך ואמר לו שפטייה שאל ממני ואתן לך
מהוני ואם אינך חפץ חפץ בממונות אנחילך קריות ומדינות שבן כתבתי לעומתך
למלאות חפצך ושאילתך והוא השיב לו בעניה ובמרי ובביכייה אם חפץ אדני
בשפטיה הנח לעוסקי תושיה ואל תוציאם מתורת יה להדיחם בצייה בתאניה ואניה
ואם אינך רוצה באלה כל כך רצוני למלא עשה בעבורי ולא יהיה שמד בעירי
והמלך בגרון קרא בחרון לולי שלחתי חותמי ונשבעתי בעצמי הייתי עושה עמך
רעה בזו העת ובזו השעה אבל מה אעשה לך שאני כתבתי אצלך ואיני יכול
לחזור בי ממה שחרטתי בכתבי ועשה לו חותם זהב נחמד שלא ישלוט בעיר
אווירי השמד ושילחו אל מקומו בכבוד לשלום לביתו ולאולמו :

אז הרשע נתן מרוצות בכל ארצות ושלח מעשים לעשות אנסים בכח לעסם
מן האמונה לאנסם[6] להשיבם להבלותו ואחרי הבלי טעותו ומשכה הירח והשמש
שנים עשרים וחמש עד יום מותו לקללה יהא אחריתו זכר עוונו ורשעתו ואל
תימח חטאתו למלכות אדום יושלם גמולו ורעתו וקילקולו להפיל שרה ממרומים
ולאבר מלכותו מהדומים לשמח ענומים לשלם לאבילים ניחומים להראותינו
ברחמים מהרה קץ הימים :

ואחר קם אחרי דורו לאון והמלך בנו בשרו יי אלהים בחרו לברכה יהא
זכרו ביטל הגזירה אשר ביזי אביו היתה גזורה והשיב היהודים לאמונתם ובחוקיהם
ובתורתם לשמור שבתותם וכל דיני מצוותם ומשפטיהם ובריתם כשהיו בקדמותם
יתברך שם משגביהם שלא עזבם ביד אויביהם והצילם משוסיהם ומלטם ממעניהם
ברוך שם אל ממרומים לעולם ולעולמי עולמים :

---

[1] So on margin by later hand.   [2] B. for N. ‏ייטן.‏   [3] K. for N.
‏כראה שהכעס והזדון.‏   [4] K. for N. ‏בעניינים.‏   [5] MS. ‏השיבו.‏   [6] MS.
‏אנסם.‏

ואחריכן החלו הישמעאלים לצאת בחיילים לשוט בגבולים במלכות עריליי
בארץ עובדי אלילים העובדים לבעלים המשתחוים לפסילים וקלברייאה שיממו
מדינותם הממו וארצותם השמו טירותם החרימו ובפולייא עברו שמה גברו ועליהם
חברו ונאונם שברו ומדינות הרבה לכדו ובזו ושדדו :

באותם הימים בבארי היה סודן מלך ישמעאלים היה באותו עידן וכל הארץ
הוא דן אז שלח מלאכים באיוירי הרשומה לעשות להם דבר קיומה ועימהם שלום
להשלימה לבלתי תת ארצם לשמה רק המס יתן להם ולא יחריב גבוליהם והוא
עשה בערמה ליל עליה פתאום להחרימה וליתנה לשמה ומשמה :

ושלח שר אויירי ו שפטייה אצלו לשמוע דברו ושיח מילולו לקבל קיומו
וכתב חותמו להיות שלימים [1] בכתב רישומו והמלך סודן בכבוד קיבלו ודברים
טובים דיבר למולו ונישאו וגידלו בפני כל השרים היושבים לקבלו ועד שבת
איחרו והוא עשה בעבורו בלי היות בה יכולת לשוב לעירו על כן לא רצה
לשגרו שלא ילך לאדונו לבשרו כשראה והבין ערמתו [2] תן לי רשות ואלך
ברשותך כי רמיתני בערמתך והוא השיבו אנה תלך בזו השעה ויום השבת קרוב
להגיע אמר לו תן לי רשות אדני זאל יהי מחשבה ממני ונתן לו רשות והלך
ובהרחיקו ממנו בעזרת שדי נמלך ובטח בשם יוצרו ועשה כמו שהאלהים עזרו
וכתב בטליפי [3] הסוס אותיות בעבור הליכתו בנחץ להיות ולהזכיר השם בנחיצה
והארץ לפניו קפצה :

ובהגיעו בתחומי ארצו צעק בכל שבילים והכריז קולו במילולים צאו בביהולים
ברחו מגבולים כי הנה סודן מלך ישמעלים עם כל החיילים לקחת הרכוש ולהפיל
חללים ולבוז בן ולשלול שללים ובקרבו שר העיר לקראתו יצא וסיפר לו שאותו
קרה [4] ומצא ונכנסו בעיצה על הדבר להתיעצה ובא אל העיר טרם חשיכה והלך
להרחיץ ברחיצה וסיכה וקיבל השבת כראוי וכהלכה בעונג במאכל ובמשתה ובשינון
הלכה ובגדים נאים להתחופף ולהסתוככה ובכל עידונים להתעדן [5] להתרככה :

וסודן וכל חילו היניחיץ בוריזות ובא עמהם בגאוה ועזות והארץ מצא מפנה
כל הארץ עד שערי המדינה וביום השבת בהגיע עת המנחה וכלא מצא כלום
רווחה נשאר בעצב ואנחה ואז ניגש אל הקירייה ושאל מר שפטיה תנו לי אותו שכפר
בתורתו וחילל שבתו ורתם נותנת להמיתו וענה ו שפטיה בדברי נאומו [6] בגבורת
אלהיו שהיתה עמו למה תדבר עוד דבריך ואין תקומה למאמר[ין] הנה בשמים
עידי וכל בני עירי מסהדי כי מבעוד יום באתי ובעוד השמש חזרתי ולבי בני
הלכתי ורחצתי וסכתי ולביתי שבתי והשבת בקדושה קיבלתי כהוגן וכראוי לי
בציווי מלכי ונואלי קדוש ישראל אלי :

---

[1] K., שלומים.   [2] No omission indicated in MS.   (N., something
missing, perhaps אמר לו בחמתו).   [3] So MS.   [4] K. for N. קרא.
[5] K. for MS. להערן.   [6] MS. נואמו.

ואבו אהרן עודנו שם הוא אהרן אשר למעלה נרשם ואז הלך לבארי המדינה
אשר על שפת הים נתונה היא הקירייה אשר נכח הים בגוייה וסורן המלך יצא
לקבלו וכבוד גדול עשה לו ושהה עמו כששה חדשים ונפלאתה לו אהבתו מאהבת
נשים וכל ימי שם היותו לא נטה מעצתו וכל מה שביקש ממנו הודיעו בבירורים
כאילו היה שואל באורים כן בכל עצתו מקויימה כל ימי היותו שמה :

והיה יום אחד בהקיץ מרדמו ורוח אלהים החל לפעמו להשיבו אל ארצו ואל
מקומו וירד הים ופנה בכל עברים נמצה אניה ¹ ערוכה ללכת למצרימה מיד עלה
וישב בתוכה והאניה בנחץ התחילה לליכה וסורן ירד בביהולה ושלח ספינות אל
האניה לחבלה והזכיר הרב השם בכח היד הגדולה ולא יכלו הספפינות להתקרב
אצלה ואבו המלחים לשוב לארץ כבתחילה והאניה להתקרב בארץ לא היתה
יכולה כראות המלך ככה חמתו כמעט שכבה כי הבין בניסי ² שהרב היה עושה
והכיר במסות שעל ידי הרב נעשות :

אז צעק המלך רבי רבי אבי אבי פרשי ורכבי למה עזבתני ולמה זנחתני קבל
מעני ושובה אדני וקח ממוני ואוצרותיי והוני ואל תזניחני בדד להניחני והוא
השיבו כשורה דרכי לפניי מישרה מאת אמיץ בגבורה ואין בי יכולת להחזירה
שאל ממני שאילתך ואגיד לך בקשתך טרם אלך מאתך ושאל ממנו דברים כמה
במניין והוא הגיד לו הכל לפי העניין ואחר שאלו בביניניבינתו אבנם והוא השיבו
תיכנס לא ברצון כי אם באונס וכמו שהשמיעו והודיעו כן הגיעו והוא הלך
בשמחה אל המנוחה ואל הנחלה אשר בארצו הניחה והגיע לביתו בנחה ³ בהשפע
וברווחה ברווח ובהצלה ונתן שבח ליוצרו לעושו וגוחו ויצרו שהשיבו לשלום
לדירו ולביתו בשמן החזירו :

אשא דעי לחוות פליאות שעל ידי ר׳ חננאל היו עשיית אח קטן היה לו
ופפוליאון שמו ובקתצר ימים נפרד מעמו וכגע יומו ונאסף ונסתם אחיו היו
בביניביבינתו לעשות מלאכתם ור׳ חננאל איחרו להוליכו בקבורת אבותיו לקברו
ויחל לאחיו עד בואם להענן ולהאנן ⁴ על אחיהם שמת לבכות ולספור ולקונן
ובעבור לא יסריח ויבאש ובשר גופו לא יבאיש כתב בקלף שם אלוה וקונו ושם
הקלף תחת לשונו והשם החייה אותו והעמידו וישב על מיטתו וסיפר שם לפניו
והיה צופה בו ומביט בעיניו ואותה ⁵ הלילה שאחיו למחר באו תמה גדול בחלום
ראו והנה מלאך יי במראה אליהם בחזון כנראה והשמיעם דברים תמיהים למה
תטריחו את יי האלהים ותעשו דברים שאינם ראויים האל ממית מחיים
ואתם לא כן תעשו את יי אלהיכם לא תנסו והם לא ידעו את אשר נעשה מן
המעשה שר׳ חננאל עשה ובהגיעם לביתם יצא לקראתם והלכו אל אחיהם לראותו
ומצאו אותו יושב על מטתו ומן המעשה לא היו יודעים ומהשם שתחת לשונו

¹ MS. אליה.   ² So MS.   ³ MS. ונחה.   ⁴ Not quite
distinct in MS.   ⁵ MS. ואותו.

אינם יודעים ושמעו כל המעשה בברר ובכו בקול יללה ומרר ועל אחיהם זעקו
לעומתו הנה גברת להחיותו ואתה תוכל להמיתו ואז הלך ר׳ חננאל בביכייה
ובמרירות ובזעקה ונאנק ואמר אל אחיו תן לי פיך ואנשקה והמת פתח פיו
ונשקהו בנשיקה והוא ידו תחת לשונו שם והשם הכתוב בקלף הוציא משם מיד
שהשם נלקח מעמו אל המטה נפל גולמו והגולם שב לעפרה ולרקבונה והנפש
הלכה אל האלהים אשר נתנה :

ואודה יי ואספר מעשה יה מן המעשה אשר להגיד ראייה שאירע באוויירי
הקירייה בבניין ה[ארמון] ¹ הנקרה הגמונייא לר׳ חננאל אחי שפטייה שהניע עצמו
לכלייה והוציאו לרווחה דר עליה ולאור הניהו מאפליה וחייבים בניו מצוקי
נשייה ליתן לשמו שבח והודייה ולומר לפניו בכל עת הללויה :

יום אחד שאלו ההגמון בעסקי דברים הכתובים באמון ומשם באו אל החשבונות
אשר במולדות תכונות ובאותו היום למחר היה חודש שישיראל ראויים לקדש
שאלו מן הלבנה בכמה שעות היא ראשונה והוא השיב לו לפי השעה ושגג וטעה
וההגמון הקשה אליו בטענה ואמר אם ככה אתה מונה הלבנה אין אתה בקי
בחשבונה ור׳ חננאל לא חישב המולד בשעה אשר הוא נולד וההגמון היה מבין
המולד כבר חישב והבין ופרש רשתו ולכדו במצודתו לולי היה בעזרתו אלהי
תשועתו וענה לו האנגמוני חננאל אם המולד כחשבוני תעשה רצוני ושוב
לדיני בספר גליוני וצא מאמונתך ומחוקי תורתך ושובה לדתי ² והאמן באמונתי
ובהבלי טעותי ואם הוא כחשבונך אמלא רצונך ואתן ³ לך סוסי מתוקן אשר
ביום הכסה לי מתוקן דמי שלש מאות זהובים ⁴ עריכתו ואם אינך חפץ בסום
תקח הדמים תמורתו וקיבלו התנאים ביניהם לקיים כל אשר יצא מפיהם בפני
השופטים ודייניהם ולפני השר המושל עליהם וצוה ההגמון באותה הלילה לעלות
אנשים על החומה ועל המגדלות לבין שעתה רגע מולדתו וחלק ראייתה וזריחתה
ור׳ חננאל בשובו לביתו שיער המולד בספירתו ומצא טעותו שסכם בקצבתו ויפג
לבו וימס בקרבו ונשמה לא נותרה בו והכין לבבו לדרוש אל יי ואל טובו אל
עזרה ⁵ הישנה שמתחילה ומראשונה נפלאותיו להראותו ומירבתי ⁶ בור להעלותו
והלך לאחיו ולכל משפחתו וסיפר להם צרתו מן המעשה שאירע אותו לפני יי
לשפוך תחינתם אולי ישמע בקול צעקתם ויעשה בכל נפלאותיו במסותיו ובאותותיו
בכמצרים הראה מופתיו אשר הפליא ועשה לאבותיו כשחשך ובא הלילה והוא
בראש גנו עלה והיה צופה למעלה למי לו השבח והגדולה ובהניע שעת הצמיחה
הלבנה באה והזריחה והוא צעק בזעקה פני שומע צעקה במרר ובצווחה בביכייה
ואנחה וחילה לדר כרובים השומע צעקת חביבים וכן אמר בתפילתו פני אלהי
תוחלתו :

¹ Suggestion of B.   ² N. לדיני.   ³ MS. ואתן.   ⁴ On
margin.   ⁵ Indistinct in MS.   ⁶ MS. ומירבתו.

אל אדון על כל העולם כל דבר ממך לא נעלם לפניך גלויייה מחשבתי כי לא
בזדון עשיתי ונסתכלתי וטעיתי ובשגגתי עשיתי ועתה אלהי תהילתי תפל נא לפניך
תפילתי וקומה לעזרתי אלהי תשועתי והנחם על שגגתי ושא נא עון חטאתי ואל
אראה בצרתי כי מחיי טוב מותי ואל תאבד מעשי ידיך וחסדך אל תרף מעבדיך
ועבור על פשע כמידת רחמיך וחסדיך וסלח נא לעווני כגודל חסדיך והאזינה
תפילתי ותחנוני וקיבל שיחי ותחן מעניי וצעקת ריגשתי ושפך חינוניי ושמע שועתי
למענך יֽי ואנשאך בועוד ישישים ואעריצך בסוד קדושים :

ויושב תהילות האזין בתפילות והלבנה נעלמה במראיתה עד הלילה האחרת
לא נראתה ובבקר הלך לקבל תנאיו וההגמון קראו לעין כל המונין ואמר לו
אתה יודע כמותי שהמולד היה בקיצבתי [1] וכחשבון ספירתי ואני לא כיזבתי ויפה
חישבתי וכן היבנתי ואמת מצאתי אבל מי יכול להעוינך [2] ואתה מתחטא בקונך
כבן מתחטא בגעגועים לפני אביו בשיפועים ונתן לו שלש מאות זהובים והוא
נתנם לעניים ולעלובים ולביתו לא הביא אחד מהם וקיבצו אחיו ואוהביו ונועדו
יחד ונתנו שבח והודיה לאל המיוחד המציל עבדו מצרה והוציאם מאפילה לאורה
ובכל עת הוא להם [3] לעזרה וסלח [4] לעמו מגן וסתרה :

אבאר המעשה שחינחתי אשר מקצת למעלה כתבתי מתופילו שכשל בעווונו
ובחנק נגמר דינו וכיצא לתחניקה כל העם יצאו לקול הצעקה ושר העיר עליהם
קפץ וההמון מעליו נפץ ואמר לו אם תצא מן האמונה ותשוב באמונתינו להאמינה
אצילך ממיתה משונה והוא כפף לו ראשו כי חס על נפשו ומיד נשאו ולארמונו
להביאו ואחר חקרו את הדברים ומצאוהו נכון באמונת העברים והשיב לו אני
עזרתיך ומיד ומיד הממיתים [5] לקחתיך ומן המות הצלתיך ואתה אלי כיזבתה וממני
לענתה [6] אני אייסרך בייסורים רעים ואכזרים משונים ועכורים התחיל להלקותו
ובחיבוט ואכזריות להכותו ויקיץ ידיו אשר עליו ועשה לרגליו ובבית האסורים
שמו ושמה עינמו [7] ואחר יהודי עמו אל אל נשא עינו משתהו ומאכלו בכל יום
מביא אצלו ואם לא היה לו הוא מביא משלו ועבדו בעצמה עד מלאת לו שנה
תמימה ובערב יום הכיפורים שעוונות עם יֽי בו מתכפרים הביא לו משתה ומאכל
והוא היהודי עמו אכל והיתה לו בת אחת קטנה ואמר לו לך והבא עדים כי לך
אתננה ענה לו אתה אדוני מן החשובים ואני אחד מן העלובים אם משפחתך
ישמעו אותי כדג יקרעו והוא ענה אין איש מושל בביתי ואין לאדם רשות בביתי [8]
ולא לבני משפחתי כי אם לבד ברשותי הלך והביא עדים שלשה ובתו לפניהם
קידשה ואמר לו לך לשלום מאתי שמהיום לא תמצא אותי ואחר הצום הלך
לדרשו ובבית האסורים ביקשו לא חי ולא מת מת אחזו כי האלהים גנזו והאלהים
ימחול לו [9] עוונותיו וכיפר לו על כל חטאותיו ותנוח נפשו באוצרותיו :

---

[1] K. for N. בקיצבתי.   [2] K. for N. להעוותך; MS. להעניתך.   [3] MS. לכם.
[4] K. for N. וסלה.   [5] K. for N. הממתים.   [6] B. for MS. לגנעתה.
[7] MS. ועיטמ.   [8] K. בבתי.   [9] N. and K. for MS. לי.

פעם אחת היה עובר ר' שפטיה ברחוב הקיריה ואותה השעה לילה היה
ושמע קול יללה בבית אחד עמיתו שהיה בעל בריתו ושמע אשה מדברת לחברתה
מספרת האחת שלמעלה אומרת לרעותה של מטה האחרת אחותי קח הילד
וקבליהו ואני ואת ביחד נאכליהו והוא האזין לדבריה והקשיב מילוליה ופתאום
הלך אליה ולקח הילד מידיה ואותם[1] הנשים לא היו בנות האנשים כי אם היו
שעירים אשר בלילה עוברים והילד הוליך לביתו והראהו לאשתו והכירו אותו
ונגנז בחדר מיטתו ואביו ואמו כל הלילה צרחו בבכיה יללה אנחו ובזעקה מרה
צווחו ובבקר הוליכוהו בבית הקברות וקברוהו והיה בשובם מהקברות ועלו לביתם
ור' שפטיה הלך אליהם כמנהג המנחמים אשר אבילים נוחמים ומתוך
דבריהם שאלם מביניהם מה חלי היה לו ואי זה פגע ביהלו וענו לו אדונינו עד
הערב ישב בינינו ואל השלחן אבל עמנו והלכנו ושכבנו על מיטתינו ובהקיצנו
משנתינו מצאנוהו מת בתוכינו וכל הלילה צעקנו ובהי ונהי יללנו ובספר קינה
קוננו ובבקר הלכנו וקברנו אותו בקברותיו אצל אבותיו אז ענה אליהם לשמח
נפשותיהם כן אני אומר לכם אינני שומע לדבריכם הוליכוני אתם בקברו[2] אשר
אתו קברתם כי בנכם[3] בקבר איננו ובחיים הוא עודינו ואל ביתכם אביאנו וחי
ושלם בעזרת אלי לכם אתננו והלכו אל הקבר וחיפשו שמה ולא מצאו כי אם
מטמא שמה אשר הבית מטאטים עמה ור' שפטיה אל ביתו שב עמהם וכל
המעשה אשר אירע סיפר להם והילד להם השיב ונתנו שבח לתפילות מקשיב
לאל היהודים מקשיב והרוח משיב :

בת היתה לר' שפטיה מאד היתה יפיפיה נאה היא ונעימה וכסיאה נקרא
שמה והיה מחבבה באהבה ובחיבה והיה אביה רוצה לזווגה ואמה לא היתה רוצה
בזיוונה שכל מי שהיה שולח ללוקחה אמה משללתו בשיחה ואומרת בדבריה
ובשיח אמריה בתי אשה חשובה ואביה גברא רבה אם כמותו לו ימצא לא
אוציאנה החוצה ואם יהיה כאביה בתורה במשנה ובמקרא בהלכה ובסברה ובסיפרי
ובסיפרא בדרשה ובגמרא בקלה וחמורה בבינה ובחכמה ברעת ובערמה ובעושר
ובגדולה באומץ וממשלה בחוקים ובמצוה בירא ה' וענה[4] ושיהיה בו כל מידה טובה :

והיה באחד ליל ר' שפטיה עמד להלל כמנהגו להתפלל תחינות נבורות ה' למלל
תושבחות ושירות לכלל קדושות ושירות לפלל תחינות לחנן לפני אל להתחנן
בזמרה לרנן בצל[5] שדי להתלונן בשירות עריבות לרוכב ערבות להחזיק ולכן
לקראת כסאו נכון ונבורתו במכון ולבטח ולשעון לאל דר במעון להדר בהילולים
לתפארתו בזבולים במצות וחוקים ליוסד ארקים לשוכן שחקים בדתי שעשועים
לכונן רקיעים בתורת יומים לאדר קולו על המים וכבודו על השמים :
ובתו מן המטה ירדה ולנגדו בחלוק אחד עמדה לעשות לו מלאכה ומים

---

[1] So MS.   [2] So MS. (N. לקברו).   [3] MS. בניכם.   [4] K. here
adds, תנה לו לאשה כתובה.   [5] K. for N. באל.

ספר יוחסין

14

לנטילת ידיו לשפכה והביט וראה שהניצו רמונים והגיעו לה העת והזמנין להתעלם
בדורים עמד והשלים תפילתו ואחר שב לאשתו בקללות לחרפה ופניה לכספה
ודיבר אליה קשות ועדות אמריו להקשות יש לי יונה תמה והיא כולה תמימה
ועת דודים הגיעו לה להיות עטרת לבעלה ואחי שאלה לחסדיה בנו להיות אצלה
ואני לקולך שמעתי ומנוחה לה לא מצאתי והכתוב במקרא חסרתי[1] ובדברי
חכמים עברתי בבקר מביתו בצאתו אל הכנסת להתפלל ברדתו לֹ חננאל אחיו
קרא והוא אליו רץ במהרה והבינו[2] רצוני וחפצי ואהבתי לחסדיה בנך לתת את
בתי כי טוב אותה לו לתתי וֹ חננאל מרוב ענוה עד ברכיו לו השתחווה
כשהשלימו התפילה זימן כל הקהילה ולביתו עמהם עלה וקידש בתו לֹ חסדיה
בן ֹ חננאל אחי ֹ שפטיה וֹ אמתיי אחי הכלה המוכללה הוא פייט היוצר
אדון מגיד מראשית אחרית בשבילה דנואי ויופי ועיטור וכתר להכלילה[3] כשזיווג
שניהם ביחד החתן עם כלה :

וֹ שפטיה זקן בא בימים וֹי בירכו בכל מידות נעימים תורה הנחילו שוכן
מרומים בעושר גדלו בנכסים עצומים בן חיסנו הגן ותמים האב והבן נמצאו
שלימים וֹ חננאל עמם בגודל ובתומים[4] בראית יֹ לעולם קיימים אחים וחביבים
בחיבוב מונעמים בתורה ובמצות עוסקים לעולמים חוקי אל באהבה מקיימים עֹז
ותפארה למלכם מרֹ[מ]מים הוד והדר לקונם מעצמים ונזר וכתר ועטרה
וברוֹאם מכתמים ליוצרם נותנים עֹז ותעצומים בֹועד התפילה מעריבים ומשכימים
הגלות והחרבן בכו בעינוגמים והשמד קוננו בתמרור ושימומים כל ימי היותם עלי
אדמים וֹמעקו וחיננו למשיב חכמים אשר בדעתו נבקעו תהומים וכונן ויוסד נהרות
וימים לסכל דעת האויב ומלכותו להשמים תבונה ביקשו למלא רחמים גזירת
השמד להאביל ולהעמים בצעקתם שצעקו לרם על כל רמים הגזירה לא עברה
מעבר הימים והציל עבדיו בתורות[י]ו תמימים מטינוף ומסריות[5] וטמים הזוהמים
מהכרעת חרשים ואלמים מהסגרת[6] עיורים וסומים מהשתחוות פסילים וצלמים
והרעים על אויביהם בקול רעמים שונאיהם ורודפיהם להזעים[7] בזעמים ומילט
ידידיו מיד הקמים וחשך נפשם מנחלי רתמים להיות בתורה עוסקים ותומים
להריחם ריח סמים ובשמים הגנוחים וחתומים באוצרות ואסמים אשר בעדן ישינים
וקדמונים ונסתם בסיתומים השלים יחידתו בשילומים לדיין אלמנות ואבי יתומים
רבי שפטיה הרב בחכמים טעם כוס הראשונים שגרם אבי פתנים לראשונים
ואחרונים :

וביום ראש השנה הוא רבי שפטיה הגן בהגובה[8] לתקוע השופר הוא בעצמו
בעבור כבוד יֹ בעמו ואותו היום מטוי מן החולי נטוי ולחשו לו כל הקהל בביטוי

---

¹ MS. חסכתי.   ² K. for N. והביט.   ³ K. for N. להכלולה.
⁴ MS. ובחומים.   ⁵ MS. ומייסריות.   ⁶ N. מהסגרת.   ⁷ N. for
MS. להנעים; K. להענים.   ⁸ So MS.

אדונינו אור עטוי זיו הודינו מאור עינינו השופר תקע אלינו כל הימים שישמרך
אלינו אין אחר תוקע שופר בתוכינו והטריחהו עליו לתקע ועמד והשופר תקע
והוא היה בלא כח ונבורה ותקיעת השופר לא בא כשורה תענה להם הצדיק ודינו
עלי הצדיק לכם בני יהיה טוב סימן כי עלי בעוני נתחלף הזמן ויצא מכנסת
עדתו והלך אל ביתו ושכב על מיטתו וכל הקהל אחריו נכנס במיטת חדריו
והוא פניו החזיר אליהם וכן אמר להם אני הולך למנוחתי לקץ הומים לגורלי
לאבות הקדומים ואודיעכם בנים חביבים בני שלשת אהובים שמת בסילי הצורר
והחובר והנהו לפני עובר בשלשלאות של אש אסור ביד מלאכי חבלה מסור
ושלח אלי יְיָ צבאות שמו לילך לקראת בסילי ולעמוד בדין עמו מכל הרעה
שעשה לעמו להכרית שמו ושם זרעו ושורשו וצאצאיו ונטעו וכתבו היום והשעה
ובימים ההם באה השמועה כי מת בסילי שעשה הרעה לפי דברי הצדיק כן הכתב
הגיע שכן מלכי קוסטנטינא עושים כמנהנ בשימות המלך משלחים בבארי בכתב
פתגם וכותבים היום והעת אשר המלך מת ונבעת[1] ברוך עושה נפלאות לבדו
אשר מזה איבדו ומהבא כיחדו ברוך שמו וברוך שם כבודו : ואני נאסף אל עמי
ואלך אל מקומי ואתם בני בחוניי בל קהל * המוניי יהי עמכם [2] יְיָ וממית
ומחיה הוא אהיה אשר אהיה בהחיותו צדיקי בנימן וגור אריה :

ויהי אחרי מות רֹ שפטיה אשר עבד אלהים בלא רמיה ועסק ברזי מרום
ובסודו כל ימי חייו לעובדו וכל ימי עודו אהב את יְיָ ועבדו בכל נפשו ובכל
מאדו ובכל לבבו ייחדו :

אחריו קם רֹ אמיתי בנו הנעים בדרכי אביו דבק והנעים ולא נטה מחוקי
יוצרו ואלהי אביו היה בעזרו וחיזק ישיבתו עם חכמי חבורתו להנות בדת אל
ותורתו שכן צוה אביו בצואתו יום אחד לפני מיתתו להקים החבורה ולנהנה
בשורה שלא יהו נפרדים החבירים והתלמידים והסיעה קבץ והמדרש ריבץ עם
הרבנים והחכמים והמבינים ואין[3] התורה לערוכה ורחבה וארוכה והיו מדוחיו
כמידות אבותיו ובמצות יְיָ ואימתו ועל החרבן נפשו עגומה והשמד בכה בנהימה
כל ימי היותו על האדמה אשר בו היתה הנשמה :

והיה יום אחד יצא לכרמו ולנחלתו החוצה ואותו היום מת אחד אכסניי חכם
ומבין ביראת יְיָ וישלחו אליו זקני העדה אל מת המצווה עימם להיוועדה ללכת
לקוברו לבכות ולספדה ולעשות לו כבוד כצווי התעודה והוא שלח אליהם אתם
מהעיר צאו ואני אייחל אתכם לד אשר תבואו ואבוא עמכם עד הקברות ואקונן
עליו קינות סדורות וכל העדה יצאו לקובריהו ורֹ אמיתי הכין ספר[4] לקוננהו
וכל הקהל בכו אותו ויקוננהו ורֹ אמיתי ספדו בקינה שעשה בעבוריהו וזו היא
ראשית הקינה שהתחיל לקוננה אי אכסניא אי גלות מי לא יכירך יעשה ממך

---

[1] K. for N. מבעת.   [2] On margin.   [3] Margin, מֹב ואין.
[4] K. for N. ספר.

הוללות ומי יבירך יקונן בילללות ושם היה עומד אחיו ר׳ משה שהתינוקות מלמד
ולחש באזני שמה עומדים מי יבירך וידעך המולים בייסורים ור׳ אמיתיי שמע
הדבר אצלו היתה שמורה ולאותו המלמד העברה נצח לו שמרה ויהי לימים רבים
וזמן הרבה ואשת איש נחשדה מאחד ריבה ונועדו העדה לעשות דרישה מן
האשה בחקירה לדרשה ולא נמצאו לאשה עדים כי אם ר׳ משה המלמד תלמידים
הוא העד לבדו ואין איש אחר נגדו ור׳ אמיתיי ענה לו בסברה יש לך עד שני
כציוותה התורה ולא נמצא עד אחר עמו והוא צוה לחזן והחרימו בתורה עשה
לעומו והשיב לו מחשבת זממו ומאוירי[1] הריחו ובגלות שילחו ובא עד מדינת
קפואה ומשם נסע והלך לפביאה:

ור׳ אמיתיי נאסף אל עמו והניח בן ועבדיאל שמו ולעבדיאל בן ושמו ברוך
ולא היה בתורה כאבותיו ערוך ובימי ברוך בביתו ספר המרכבה היה שבו שמש
כל ימי חייו ר׳ שפטיה והיה יום אחד בערב שבת שבו אל מכל מלאכתו שבת
והיום חשכה והאורה חשכה ולא היה שהנר מדליק לפני ספר המרכבה להדליק
ואשה אחת עמדה היא הארורה היתה נידה מספר החיים תהא אבודה ומהעולם
הבא תהא כתודה הדליקה הנר לפני התורה ואף י׳ במשפחה חרה וימותו במגפה
רבים ונשארו מעט מהרבים ושם היה יהודי אחד אחר מבין המעשה הכיר והבין ולקח
הספר ובכלי אבר שמו ואל המצולה לשקעו והים גם לאחורה כשיעור מיל אחד
היתה החזרת והיהודי השליך הכלי לימה שבה והים שבה אל מקומה ומיד בטלה
הגזירה והמגפה נעצרה וזכר ברוך נשבת ורו נדעך ונכבת שלא הניח עוסק
במשיבה ולא היה לו בן כי אם אחת בת:

ולר׳ חסדיה ביר׳ חננאל היה בן ושמו פלטיאל ור׳ פלטיאל הוליד בן ושמו ר׳
חננאל ובת אחת ושמה כסיאה את י׳ היא מאד יריאה ותלד בן ושמו ר׳ פלטיאל
בכוכבים יודע להבין:

ויהי בימים ההם והישמעאלים יצאו בחייליהם ואלמעוז[2] קייט עליהם ועברו
איטליאה והרסו כל הארץ קלבריאה ובא עד אוירי אשר בקצה פוליה ויצורו
עליה והשמידו כל חייליה ותבוא העיר במצור ולא היה כח באנשי המדינה לעצור
והעיר הובקעה והחרב עד הנפש נגעה והרגו רובם והנשארים הוליכו בשבייה
והקייט שאל ממשפחת ר׳ שפטיה ושלח אליהם והביאם לפניו וי׳ נתנם לרחמים
בעיניו והאלהים הטה חסדו על ר׳ פלטיאל עבדו ונתנו בחין[3] מעין נגידו והוליכו
באהלו תעימו ניהלו לעמוד לפניו לשרת לו:

ובלילה אחת הקייט ור׳ פלטיאל יצאו להביט בכוכבים והביטו וראו והנה כוכב
הקייט[4] ושלשה כוכבים בלעה ולא ביחד כי אם זה אחר זה שלשתם
ושאלו אלמעוז מה היבנתה בבינה והוא השיב אתה תאמר ראשונה ענה הקייט

¹ MS. ומאורי.   ² MS. ואל מעוז.   ³ MS. בחין; N. (כהן) בהין.
⁴ K. suggests insertion of הופיע.

הכוכבים הם שלש מדינות טרנטו ואודרנטו ובארי שאני עתיד לקנות ענה ה'
פלטיאל לא כן אדוני כי דבר גדול ראיתי אני הכוכב אחד תמלוך באיסקילאה
והשנית תמלוך באפריקאה והשלישית תמלוך בבולוניאה מיד חיבקו ועל ראשו
נשקו והסיר טבעתו ולו נתנו ושבועה נשבע למענו ואמר אם כן כדבריך וייאמנו
מאמריך אתה תהיה על ביתי ומושל בכל מלכותי ובכל ממשלתי :

ועד לא מלאת ימים שבעה ואלמעזו הגיעה השמועה ושלחו לו השרים אשר
באיסקילאה דרים דע שמת האמירה ואתה תבוא בנחץ ובמהרה וקבל הממשלת
זהשררה [1] בכן קיבץ חיילותיו ונכנס בספינותיו עם כל ראשי גייסותיו ועבר אליהם
ומלך עליהם אז האמין ובדברי ה' פלטיאל היה מאמין ולא נטה מעצתו לא
לשמאל ולא לימין והשליטו בביתו ועל מלכותו ובכל ממשלתו והוא היה משרתו
ועושה שירותו :

ואחרי כן עלה באפריקיאה ואחיו הניח מושל סקיליאה וה' פלטיאל עמו עלה
ושם גבר ונתעלה ושמו עולה למעלה והוא היה משנה למלך ושמעו בכל
המדינות הולך :

בימיו שלח מלך אדום פני מלך אפריקיאה במנחה לקדום והשליח בא בטכסיסין
כמו שהיונים עושים ושאל מי פקיד בית המלכות ומי מנהג הנסיכות ענה לו אחד
ערבי יהודי הוא המוציא והמביא והוא מושל בכל ארצו ואין המלך יוצא מחפצו
והמלך אין איש יכול לראותו ולא ליכנס לביתו וללכת לקראתו כי אם ברצון
היהודי וברשותו והיווני בנאוותו בעזותו וביהירותו בשטותו ובחוסר דעתו השיב
ענה טרם אלך מזו המדינה ואעלה לקוסטנטינא אל אדוני אשר שלחני הנה ועם
היהודי לא אתחבר עמו אל המלך לדבר ולפני ה' פלטיאל הדברים הגיעו וכל
המעשה לו הודיעו וגזר וצוה בחצר המלך ארוחת ומשאת איליו בלי לילך ובמקום
נטע אהלו אדם פניו בלי להקבילו ושהה כעשר ימים [2] בקצף בחרון ובזעמים
ואחר שב בניאומים לבקש מחילה ורחמים [3] לבל יזכור שטותו והבלו והפשע
והעוון למחול לו מאשר העווה לו בסכלו ואשר שגג במילולו ואז שלח אליו
לבוא ומנעו באותו היום לפניו מבוא ויהי ביום השלישי לפניו הביאו וכיבדו
והדרו וגדלו ונשאו במתנות עצומים במוסקו ואהלות ורוב בשמים באבני יקרה
ושהם לשמים [4] ובתכשיטי מלכות החמודים והנעימים וכבוד גדול עשה לו מפתח
שער היכלו ועד מקום סעודת מאכלו בבגדי שיריין ומלתין תיקן כל הפלטים
ובתולעת שני ובבגדי משי ותכשיטים יסוד קרקע החצר וקירות הבית מקושטים
על השיריאן כף רגלו דרכה ועליהם צעד נתיבתו בהליכה ומצא היווני ה' פלטיאל
במסיבה יושב ולעצמו מצא קתדרא זהב לישב וישב ונכנס עמו בדברים ושאלו
מתורת העברים ומייחוסו וממשפחתו ומארץ מולדתו והשיבו תשובות תכונות [5]

צרופות ובחונות וצוה להביא מים לנטילת ידים ופה בקיתון וספל שלשהם וישפה
ובסתר צוה לשברו לאחר נטילת ידו והעבד עשה כציווי אדונו הביא הספל
וקיתונו ונתן המים על ידי רבונו ואחר המים על ידיו כנותנו[1] נפל לפני רגליו
וישבר הכלים לפניו והיווני קם בבהלה ואחזתו חלחלה ומראה פניו נשתנה ועוז
פניו שונה ור פלטיאל פניו למולו שחק ולפני כל העומדים שם צחק ואמר ליווני
למה נבהלת ובבהל ממקומך עמדת ענה לו השליח היווני כי הפסד גדול ראיתי
אני ואין ערך ותמורה אל הקיתון והספל שנשברה אז שאלו ממלך אדומים בכלי
זהב משתמשים או ביהולמים[2] וענה השליח המקדוני בכלי זהב משתמשים בבית
אדוני השיב לו אדונך איש חסרונים שכלי יקר ופנינים יקרים מכלי זהב בדמים
שהכלים של אבן יקרה אין להם תקנה בשבירה וכלי זהב אם להם שברון מתקנים
אותם בלי חסרון וכמות הכלים שראיתה שנשברו בביתי עתה בבית אדוני המלך
נשברים ואחרי כל זאת בכבוד שילחו אל מלך אדום אשר שלחו :

ור חננאל בן פלטיאל שאל רשות ממלך אפריקיאה לעבור הים ולרדת
באיטליאה שבשעת שהיה באוירי הגלות והשיבייה הנשארים נמלטו בבארי
ובאודרינטו הוליכו עמהם ממטלטלי בתיהם וממון אחירים שאינו שלהם הצילו עם
ממוניהם ועלה ר חננאל לקוסטנטינא ובנפש אנונה ומרה ועגונה מאת המלך ביקש
תחינה למצוא פניו חנינה לעשות לו חותם מלכותו ללכת בכל מדינות ממשלתו
ובכל מקום שימצא ממטלטלי ביתו להיות ברשותו ובחזקתו וקיבל החותם וירד
לבארי המדינה ומצא שם מדבר שלו אחת מקרא ישנה ותכשיטי בגדי נשים
ומעילים תפורים שהם מלבישים[3] והיו רבי חכמי בארי טוענים לו בטענה המציל
מן הנויים[4] מן הנהר ומדליקה שלו הם בנתינה שכן הורה ר בהוראת המשנה
והוא השיב להם כן הוא באמונה אבל הורו רבותינו דינא דמלכותא דינא והנה
הכתב עם החותם אשר המלך לי חתם וביצעו עמו ונתנו לו המעילים והמקרא
והניח להם הנשאר בפשרא[5] ועד ביניבינטו ירד וכל הקהל לקראתו חרד וישב
שם שנה תמימה ואחרי כן קבע ישיבתו שמה[6] ולקח משם אשה אסתר שמה
בת ר שבתי ממשפחת ר אמיתי ומטה כלפי חסד כמידת טובתו נכמרו רחמיו
וחמלתו זכר חסדו ואמונתו לבית ר שפטיה ור חננאל אנשי סגולתו אשר
בעבודתו כל ימי חייהם לא משו מתורתו[7] שכן היא אמונתו להטיב למצפי
ישועתו ולמייחלי עזרתו והנחילו בנים הגונים בזקונותו ר שמואל בכורו כוחו
וראשיתו ור שבתי ופפוליאון וחסדיה חסדיה עלה עם ר חננאל באפריקיאה אצל
ר פלטיאל בן אחותו כסיאה ור שמואל בא בקפואה העירה ושם נשה אשה ושמה
אלבאבירה אחרי כן עלו ר שבתי ופפוליאון עם המנחה אשר לר פלטיאל מאת

---

[1] בנותנו .K. for N.   [2] So MS.   [3] מלבושים .K. for N.
[4] הגוים .N.   [5] בפרשה .N.   [6] עמה .K. for N.   [7] N. and K.
תורתו for MS.

שר אמלפי שלחה והם כמנהג הנערים נכנסו עם קבירנים הספינה בדברים
ויאמרו נעשה שם ונלך בבהלה ונהיה אל מחוז אפריקיאה בזו הלילה וכתבו
והזכירו שם שוכן מרומה והשליכו הכתב בתוך מי הימה ואמרו למלחים הזהרו
בנו כעצמה לבל היות לנו תנומה וגרם החט[א] והעם ואשמה ונפלה עליהם
שנת תרדמה והרוח סיערם על פני המימה ונהפכה הספינה וירדו האנשים בעימקי
תהומה וכח השם הוליך הספינה באיספמיא ובנרבונא וגם בים קוסטנטינא והחזירה
לאחור עד ים אנקונא ואחר שיברה באמלפי המדינה :

יימת מלך מצרים ושלחו זקני מצרים ספרים מרשות הסגנים והחורים והעם
היושבים במדינות ובכפרים ביד צירים נאמנים שליחים חכמים ונבונים אלמען
מלך התימנים שמענו נבורותיך וחזק מלחמותיך אשר נלחמת בחכמתך וגברת
בערמתך על המלכים קדמונים שהיו ראשונים במלכות סוינים [1] עתה עלה אלינו
ותהיה מלך עלינו בעצת שרינו וכל נדולי ארצינו ואנחנו עבדיך ואתה מלכינו :

אז נכנס במחשבה ור׳ פלטיאל לפניו הובא ובעצה נכנסו לדעת מה יעשו כי
הדרך היתה רחוקה ומדבר וארץ צרה וצוקה ואין בכל הדרך מים ומזונות ולא
אהלים ובית מלונות ועבר ר׳ פלטיאל לפניו ועשה מחנות ותיקן שווקים ובית
לינות והושיב בהם תגרים והושיב בהם לחם ומים ודנים ובשר וירקי גנות וכל
דבר הנצרך לחיילים הבאים מהמדינות ועלה המלך והשרים והגדולים וקבעו
המחנות והאהלים רחוק ממצרים שלשה מילים וכל שועי מצרים יצאו בריצה
והפרתמים והפחות בעליצה והשליטים והנדיבים וכל דלת העם בדיצה ויבאו
לפניו וישתחו לו אפיים ארצה ובחוקי דתם השביעם ולקח בני התערובת מקציני
העם ונכנס ר׳ פלטיאל במצרים עם מקצת החיילות וערך החומות והמגדולות
ושמרו המדינה ובית המלכות והיכלות והפקיד שומרים לשמור ימים ולילות רוב [2]
פאתיו וכל נבולות ואחרי כן נכנס המלך עם כל חילו ונקבצו השרים וכל העם
באו אצלו וכולם שנית נשבעו לו ועלה אל החצר וישב בהיכלו על כסא מלכותו
ותפארתו וגודלו ושמו בידו השרביט וכתר מלכות בראשו ומלך במלכות הנגב
ככל אות נפשו :

והיה ביום הכיפורים [3] נקרא ר׳ פלטיאל לקרוא בתורה ויקומו ויעמדו מלפניו
כל החבורה והחכמים והמבינים היושבים בשורה הבחורים והזקינים והנערים
הקטנים והטפים והילדים כל הקהל היו עומדים אז צעק אליהם ואמר לכולהם
ישבו השבים [4] ויעמדו הרובים [5] ואם אין אין אשוב ואשב כי אין בעיני מתחשב לאחר
השלים קרייתו נדב לאלהי תהלתו חמשת אלפים דינרים טוב [6] שלימים ונמורים
אלף לראש הישיבה ולחכמים ואלף לאבילי בית העולמים ואלף לבבל לישיבת
הנאונים ואלף אל קהילות לעניים ולאביונים ואלף לכבוד התורה לקנות שמנים

---

[1] So MS.   [2] K. for רום פאתי.   [3] On margin.   [4] MS. הסבים.

[5] On margin, פי׳ כמו רביא כלו׳ הקטנים.   [6] So MS.

ובבקר השכים והקדים כי לעולם במצוה הזריז מקדים לבל יתקפו יצרו מדרך
טובה להחזירו והביא רוכבי סוסים ופרדים ונתן להם גדולים ושילחם עם השיירות
ההולכים המדברות והוליכו הזהובים בידיהם כציווי ה׳ פלטיאל אדוניהם וחילקום
כמצות ה׳ פלטיאל לישיבות ולכנסיות ולאביליי ציון ולעניי קהילות ישראל :

ופרשת גדולותיו אשר גדלו המלך באורצרותיו והשליטו במלכות מצרים וממלכת
ארמים עד ארם נהריים ובכל ארץ ישראל עד ירושלם וממשלתו ותוקפו
ועושרי אשר נשאו המלך והידרו הלה הם רשומים על ספר דברי הימים למלכות
נף וענמים :

ואלמעוֹ[1] חלה את חליו אשר מת בו והמליך את בנו ושם אותו ביד ה׳
פלטיאל חביבו להיות לו לעיצה לעזרה ולשמירה ולנהג המלכות באומץ ובגבורה
וימת המלך וישכב אם אבותיו וימלך בנו תחתיו ויהיו כל ימיו בשקט ובבמחה
בשלום והנחה :

ויהי בשבתו על כסא מלכותו והיו השלטונים אשר על מלאכת מצרים ממונים
למלך היו מאזינים על ה׳ פלטיאל דברו ריגונים[2] ובחרב לשונם שונגים ובכל יום
עליו בסתר מלשינים והמלך חמתו בם בוער ותמיד גם נוער ולֹי פלטיאל הנגיד
כל דבריהם היה מגיד ונתייעצו ביניהם מה לעשות להם יצא ה׳ פלטיאל הוא
ואשתו עם כל אנשי ביתו ואוהביו ועבדיו וכל משפחתו לשדהו ולנחלתו לפרדסו
ולגינתו אשר נתן לו המלך במתנתו :

והמלך שאל בתמידות[3] אנה הלך איש חמודות ה׳ פלטיאל מבין סודות וענו
לו העבדים אשר בחצר עומדים יצא נפשו לשמחה עם אוהביו ובני ביתו לשמחה
אל גינת הביתן אשר המלך לו נתן וישלח המלך לקרוא לשלטוניו ויקרא לשריו
ולסגניו ויאמר להם המלך אני ואתם נלך ונקביל פני פילוסופוס הזקן המשרת
לפני הוא ה׳ פלטיאל הנחמד והיקר הנכבד בעיניי וירכב במרכבתו וכל קציניו
ורמוניו הוליך איתו והמלך עשה בחכמה וכל המעשה היתה בערמה כי יציאת ה׳
פלטיאל היתה במרמה מפי המלך היתה שומה לגלגל הדבר להראות לו חיבה
עצומה בפני כל המוניי ושרי אומה[4] להלבין שוטניו ופניהם להעטותם[5] בושת
וקלון וחרפה והמלך הולך וקרב באהל ה׳ פלטיאל מתקרב וגזר שלא ילך אדם
להגיד לו עד שהגיע המלך באהלו וירד המלך מן המרכבה וה׳ פלטיאל לפניו
בא וחיבקו מרוב חישקו והיה מנפפו ומנשקו ואחזו בידיו והלכו שניהם יחדיו
וישבו הם לבדם וכולם עמדו במעמדם ויבאו המשחקים והמתופפים ויקחו בידם
הכינורים והתופים וישחקו לפניהם בעוגב ומינים ושירים בתוף ומצלתים בנבל
עשור מזמרים מהבוקר ועד פנות היום לאחר צהריים עד עת הערב כנטות הצל
לאחוריו וירכב המלך וישב למצרים וילך ונתכרכמו פני השוטנים ונכלמו האויבים

[1] MS. ואת מעוֹ.   [2] K. ריגונים.   [3] K. for N. בחמודות.
[4] MS. עומה.   [5] MS. להטעותם.

והמשטינים ובאותו היום פיהם נאלם [1] ולא לדבר עליו רעה לעולם ברוך שומר
חסדיו הפודה ומציל נפש עבדיו ברוך הוא וברוך שמו ברוך כבוד יֹי ממקומו:
והיה בליל אחד יצא ר׳ פלטיאל [עם המלך] החוצה ויחזו והנה שלשה כוכבים
אדירים נאספו ובשעה אחת נגהם [2] אספו ויאמר ר׳ פלטיאל הכוכבים החשיכים
הם שלשה מלכים אשר בשנה זו מתים ובקרוב הם נצמתים המלך האחד חוני [3]
היוני והשני מלך בגדד הצפוני וימהר המלך להשיבו באוני השלישי אתה מלך
תימני ויען למלך אל אדוני כי אני יהודי והמלך השלישי הספרדי והשיב לו המלך
דְאוֹמֵר אתה השלישי באמת כמו שאני אומר:
ובאותה השנה מת ר׳ פלטיאל המנגד [4] לקהילות עם אל הדרים במצרים ובארץ
ישראל בפלירמו ובאפריקאה ובכל ממשלת ישמעאל כי הוא רודה במלכות
הערבים [5] ובמלכות ארמים והמצרים ומלכות ישמעאלים וארץ ישראלים בצרור
החיים נפשו תהא צרורה בעדן שמורה בן אלהים אצורה אצל האבות סדורה:
ויקם ר׳ שמואל בנו תחתיו איש גדול ונכבד בדורותיו ממלא היה מקום
אבותיו והעלה אביו ואמו בירושלם בארונות ועצמות ר׳ חננאל דוד אביו שבארן
נתונות ועצמות אשר בבלסמון [6] מתוקנות והקדיש לדר [7] עליונים ולהיות לו צדקה
מאת רוכב עננים מזהב עשרים אלף דרכמונים לדלים ועניונים לחכמים והדרשנים
אשר התורה משננים ולמלמדי תינוקות וחזנים ושמן למקדש בכותל מערבי למזבח
שבפנים ולבתי כנסיות לקהלות הרחוקים והשכינים ולאבילי ההיכל המשכנים [8] הם
העגומים על ציון ואבילים ואל הישיבה לתלמידים ולתנאים ולחכמי בבל לישיבת
הנשיאים זכרו יהא לברכה ו[י]חידתו תהא תמוכה בסעד חיים ערוכה באוצרות
אלהים סמוכה:
אתן [9] צדק לאלי שבח וגדולה למחוללי ארומם בשיר מלולי אלהים יֹי חילי
בתוך ועד קהילות לשמו אביע תהילות באימה ומורא לחלות פני עושה גדולות
גדולת כבודו לרוממה גבורת תוקפו לקוממה בחיך וגרן אנעימה דרוש מעשיו
המפוארים נצח מלכותו ארים דרוך נתיבותיו במישרים לעדי עד לדורי דורים
הלל ועוז ורננה אפציח בגיל ורינה הדרת אלי מעונה אזכיר בכל עת ועונה
ואומץ מופתים וניסים הראה בכל אפסים ונואי [8] כשרון מעשים יישר לבניו
עמוסים זכר רחמיו וחסדיו לזרע שני ידידיו זכות וצדקות חסידיו הממציא לבית
עבדיו חשכם [10] מזעם ועברה והצילם מצרה וצוקה חיבבם חיבה יתירה מילתם [11]
מרועה גזירה נגזרה מיכסם יקרה מפנינים המתוקה מדבש בגרונים טהור עיניו בנאמנים

---

[1] MS. נלאם. [2] MS. נהגם. [3] K. for N. חמי; on margin,
ס׳ אֹ רומי. [4] MS. המנגן; K. המנגד. [5] N. for MS. העברים. [6] K. כבלסמון.
[7] Inserted by K. [8] So MS. [9] Beginning double alphabetical
acrostic, pointed out by K., not indicated by N. [10] MS. חסכם.
[11] N. for MS. מילנים.

סיפקם וכילכלם במזונם יושבי באווירי באיולים בשבעה עשר יובלים ירד מלך
ישמעאלים הרחיקם מעל גבולים כעס ובחרון נתעבר וקלבריאה הרס ושיבר
כיבש מן המעבר ובארץ לונגוברדריאה גבר לחץ הארץ בחזקה והביאה ברוחק
ובצוקה לארצו הגלה בבוקה נפשם וחיתם לשבקה[1] מרום שוכן שחקים המביט
ומרעיד עמקים מצווה ונחר ומקים כל אדני ארץ ארקים נתן בעיני[ו] לרחמים
בני עבדיו התמימים נזכר להם מרמומים זכות אבות הקדמונים סקר מלך בבינה
וראה ביניהם בתבונה סבר בכוכבים להבינה יודע בחכמות להתבוננה עילו על
חכמיו ומסר בידו אסמיו עצמו היהודים בימיו כמלאת הירדן במימיו פקיד ונגיד
ממונה בבית המלך משנה פועלים מנכסיו מהנה המימים והכופרים מענה צלח
והאדיר בגדולתו ורחבה וארכה מתנתו צמחו[2] נדבתו וברכתו לאוהבי יّ ותורתו
קודש וחילק ממונות לעניי ירושלם והמדינות קדם לישיבות התכונות ולחכמים
וליודעי בינות רד מחלציו נקי ממולא בתורה ובקי רומם[3] בוגד וצדוקי[4] עזר
וממלט איןקי שוקר על המטובה לעבוד יّ באהבה שמר מצוותיו בחיבה בנפש
חפיצה ותריבה תם ונודב נדבות לנאותו ועזו בערבות תמך[5] תלמידי הישיבות
ולחזק נדכאי לבבות. אהבה[6] שלימה וגמורה. חיבה יתירה ועצומה. ידעם[7] אל
נורא. מדע והשכל וסברה. עצה ודעת וגבורה. צמדם עוטה אורה. בינה
וחכמה ותורה. ריבוץ עושר ותפארה. בירכם דר נהורה. יראה וענוה טהורה.
פיקודים ודרך ישרה. ליבבם עולם ברא. טוב מכסף סחרה. יותר מפנינים
יקרה. איפרם עונה בצרה. לפליטת קדושים הנשארה. חזוק וממשלת ושררה
אימץ ברוחו שמים שפרה לצאצאימו וניהגם בשורה ועליהם היה מגן וסתרה
חומה נשגבה ועיר בצורה מגדל עז לבניהם ומחסה ועזרה טרף נתן להם הירבה
והרחיב גבוליהם בירך מעשה ידיהם בירכתו באוצרותיהם ושלום ובטח
בבתיהם ושקט ושלוה באהליהם וריווח והצלה בקינייניהם :

כשהגיעו בקפואה נין[י]הם נתנם יّ אלהיהם לרחמים לפני שלטוניהם והעלו
שלטוני המדינה ר שמואל בארמוניהם והפקידו אותו[8] על בית גיניזיהם להיות
מושל במדינה שלהם על מחוז הנהר ומכס שווקיהם על המטבע בנימוסי העיר
ודימוסיהם ואלהי אבותינו עזרו והוא היה בעזרו ועלה אצל ר פלטיאל פעמים
ונתן לו חפצים טובים ובכל פעם ופעם ימים ויّ מסביב הניחו ובתורת שעשועים
שימחו ובנכסים הצליחו עשות ספרים הרבה עסק בכל כוחו ובניינים בנה לדירת
שבחו ובן הנון נתן לו האל ושם שמו ר פלטיאל הולך בדרכי אל ודובק בתורת
ישראל מדרכי אביו לא סר והחזיק בידאת יّ בחכמה ובמוסר וכל טוב יّ מביתו
לא חסר ומינהו בביתו המושל והשר[9] וכל שירות המדינה בידו מסר ועל

---

[1] Or לשנקה (N.). [2] K. for N. צמחו. [3] MS. רומם.
[4] MS. צדיקי. [5] K. for N. תמחוי (MS. תמוי). [6] Beginning of
nominal acrostic. [7] N. for MS. יירעה. [8] N. for MS. אותם.
[9] N. for MS. והסר.

פקידי [1] שוע וסבר ושפטים ושטרים ונגשים כל דבר ועל כולם הוא היה נגזר
ומוציא ומביא ומנהיג ודבר ודבק בחוקי יי ובתורתו ואהב מצוותיו ומשפטי דתו
בכל לבו לעבדו ובכל נפשו לייחדו ותיקן כנסת זקינו לבית תפילה לכבוד שוכן
מעלה והיה לו חסרן בנים כי הבנים שהיו לו נולדים בשתים ושלש שנים היו
מתים כשהן קטנים והיה דווה בדאבונים ומתענג בעינונים והיון בחינונים פני שוכן
מעונים ויתפלל אל יי ויעתר לו וישמע תפילתו ושוועת קולי והאזין תחינתו משמי
זבולו וברחמיו וחסדיו בן יחיד הנחילו ור אחימעץ קרא שמו בבית הספר שמו
לקרוא בתורה ולהגות במקרא ביראתו הטהורה במצוותו ברה בעידות נאמנה
פיקודיו לבוננה :

ואני אחימעץ ביר פלטיאל ביר שמואל ביר חננאל ביר אמיתי עבד אל
בחדש אחד [2] ברבים [3] שנים למפיחת שמים תחינה מאת מדד בשעלו
מים להחכימני [4] בסוד רזי שעשוע יומיים לאמצני בתורתו התמימה אלפיים שנה
היתה קדומה להדריכני בדרך ישרה לחזקני ולהיות לי לעזרה להאזין תביעת
בקשותי לסעדני למצוא ייחוס אבותיי ועיניי אליו נשאתי ובשם קדשו בטחתי
וברחמיו ביקשתי וחסדיו שאלתי ויתן לי את שאלתי אשר מאתו חמדתי וחישבתי
ובינותי ואת שאהבה נפשי אחזתי וייחוסי מצאתי ובאלי התחזקתי וסדר ערכתי
וחרז תיקנתי ומראש התחלתי מגלות ירושלם וחרבן בית תפארתי וגלות אווירי
קריית חנייתי ועד ביאת אבותיי בקפואה היגעתי ובדורי ובדור בני נחתי
בספר כתבתי וקבצתי ואגרתי ואגדתי [6] לדורות הבאים אחריי איסםתי מפורש
גליתי והינחתי [7] ולאלי שיבחתי ונאווה ועוז הידרתי ולפני כבודו פאר ושבח
רוממתי שעזרני לגמור ספר קיצבתי ובחדש סיון אותו סיימתי במזל תאומים
שבו ניתנה תורתנו בעת תם קץ בכפל בבקשתי מראשו ועד סופו כולו נמרתי
יתברך יקר כבוד שכינתו והדרת כם תפארתו ויתעלה שמו ושם כבוד מלכותו :

אחשבה לדעת מספר ימיהם מדור לדור לדעת מידת שנותיהם מימי ר שפטיה ור
חננאל ועד ימי רבי אחימעץ ביר פלטיאל השמד שעשה בסילי המגונה היה בשנת
ארבעת אלפים ושש מאות ועשרים ושמונה ור שפטיה ור חננאל באותו הזמן חיו
ואחרי מות ר חננאל [8] בנו ר חסדייה ור חסדיה הוליד ר פלטיאל ור פלטיאל
הוליד רבי חננאל ובשנת ארבעת אלפים ושבע מאות עלה ר שמואל בנו בעזרת
אדון הפלאות ובששים ושמונה ושמונה השלים יחידתו לאלהי צבאות ובשבע מאות
וארבעים ושמונה ושמונה נולד ר פלטיאל בנו ושמנה מאות ושלש מסר נפשו לקנו
ובשבע מאות ושבעים ושבע נולד ר אחימעץ חמודו יושב הכרובים יהיה בעזרתו
ובסעדו ויאריך שנותיו למען כסא כבודו ובשבע מאות ותשעים [9] ושמונה נולד

---

[1] N. for MS. פקיד ישוע‎; (‏.K) פקיד ושוע‎).   [2] N. אדר‎.   [3] N. בְּרֻבִֹּם‎.
[4] K. for N. להחכימי‎.   [5] N. for MS. ביקשתי‎.   [6] K. for N. reading
twice in MS. ואגרתי‎.   [7] K. והינהתי‎.   [8] K. here adds עלה‎.
[9] N. for MS. ועשרים‎; K. ח‎ כ‎, perhaps פ‎"ח‎.

בנו ר׳ פלטיאל ובשמונה מאות וארבע נתן לו יי בן שיני ושמו ר׳ שמואל יחיים
האל אלהי ישראל ובימיהם יבנה ההראל ובית המקדש הקראוי אריאל ויצמח
גואל הוא מנחם בן עמיאל ונחמיה בן חושיאל נפוצי בית יעקב להיקבץ ולהיגאל
בקרוב בימינו ובימי כל בית ישראל אמן :

בשנת ארבעת אלפים ושמונה מאות וארבע עשרה לבריאת עולם אשר ברא
הבורא אספתי זה ספר יוחסי בעזרת יֹי מנוסי ולא מחכמה שבי והסכל שסביבי
ומתבונה שבחובי כי אם ממה שחינני אל אלהים אדוני :

ברוך נותן ליעף כח ולאין אונים פקחקוח :

נשלם ביד מנחם ביר׳ בנימן

יעזרם בורא שמאל וימין :